HISTORIC  SCOTLAND

MEDIEVAL SCOTLAND

HISTORIC SCOTLAND

MEDIEVAL SCOTLAND

AN ARCHAEOLOGICAL PERSPECTIVE

PETER YEOMAN

B. T. Batsford Ltd / Historic Scotland

For Sarah

First published 1995

Typeset by DP Press Ltd

Printed and bound in Great Britain by
Butler & Tanner Ltd, Frome and London

Published by B. T. Batsford Ltd
4 Fitzhardinge Street, London W1H 0AH

A CIP catalogue record for this book is available from
the British Library

ISBN 0 7134 7465 3 (limp)
     0 7134 7464 5 (cased)

Contents

Illustrations

Colour plates

Acknowledgements

If ever a book was a collaborative effort, then this is it. This is a testament to the dedicated skills of a small number of Scottish medieval archaeologists, notably Gordon Ewart, John Lewis, David Caldwell and Derek Hall, who generously supplied me with data, explanations and illustrations. I am very grateful to them, and to Adrian Cox, Catherine Smith, Rosemary Cramp, Richard Fawcett and Chris Tabraham, for advice and comments on parts of the text. I am also indebted to the following for their unstinting assistance: W. Cormack, Steve Driscoll, David Bowler, Hugh McBrien, Bob Will, Piers Dixon, Judith Stones, Hilary and Charlie Murray, Peter Hill, Jerry O'Sullivan, John Barber, Mike Spearman, Nick Bogdan and the late Ian Smith. I am grateful to David Breeze of Historic Scotland and Peter Kemmis Betty and Charlotte Vickerstaff of Batsford, for their patient encouragement during the creation of this book.

I have relied heavily on reconstruction drawings to evoke the reality of the past, and these have chiefly been produced by Alan Braby, David 'Rat' Connelly and David Pollock. Obtaining illustrations has been a nightmare from which I have been rescued by Joe White, Mike Brooks and David Henry (Historic Scotland); Lesley Ferguson and colleagues (Royal Commission on the Ancient and Historical Monuments of Scotland); Richard White (Aberdeen Art Gallery and Museums); Ann MacSween (AOC Scotland Ltd); Sue Payne (Perth Museum); Ian Shepherd (Grampian Regional Council) and John Dent (Borders Regional Council). Special thanks are offered to Mike King, and to Perth Museum, for granting me access to the illustrations and research compiled for their marvellous exhibition entitled 'Mud, Muck, and Middens of Medieval Perth'. Interminable editing was eased by the keyboard skills of Angie Wilkie.

Much of the research was compiled during a leave of absence kindly granted by Fife Regional Council, and I am grateful to W.G. Taylor, Director of Economic Development and Planning, for his encouragement. I owe a great deal to Sarah Govan and Rob Terwey, who picked up the pieces during my absence. Above all I am pleased to acknowledge the financial support I received from the Russell Trust and the Rosemary Cramp Fund, which made my leave of absence possible.

I am grateful to the following for their kind permission to reproduce photographs and illustrations: AOC Scotland Ltd (**28**); Aberdeen Archaeological Surveys – Crown Copyright (**74, 91**); Mick Aston (**colour plate 16**); Alan Braby (**16**); City of Aberdeen Art Gallery and Museums Collections (**33, 35, 47, 54, 55, 60, 61, 64, 72, 79, 93, colour plates 4, 5, 11, 13**); W. Cormack (**26, 27**); Fife Regional Council (**2, 8–10, 11, 45, colour plate 1**); Glasgow University Archaeological Research Division (**13, 15, 30, 31, colour plate 8**); Crown Copyright: Royal Commission on the Ancient and Historical Monuments of Scotland (**13, 18, 23, 94, colour plates 3, 14, 15**); Scottish Urban Archaeological Trust Ltd (**19, 40–2, 44, 49, 50–3, 58, 65, 66, 70, 101, colour plates 6, 9**); Borders Regional Council (**22, 90**); National Museums of Scotland (NMS) (**97**), NMS and Marion O'Neil (**98**); Paisley Museum and Art Gallery (**14**); Perth High Street Archaeological Committee and Nick Bodgan (**37, 46, 56, 68, 69, colour plate 12**); Perth Museum and Art Gallery (**32, 34, 36, 38, 39, 43, 48, 67, 71, 92, colour plate 10**); David Pollock (**59**); Rosemary Cramp (**24, 25**). All other illustrations are copyright Historic Scotland.

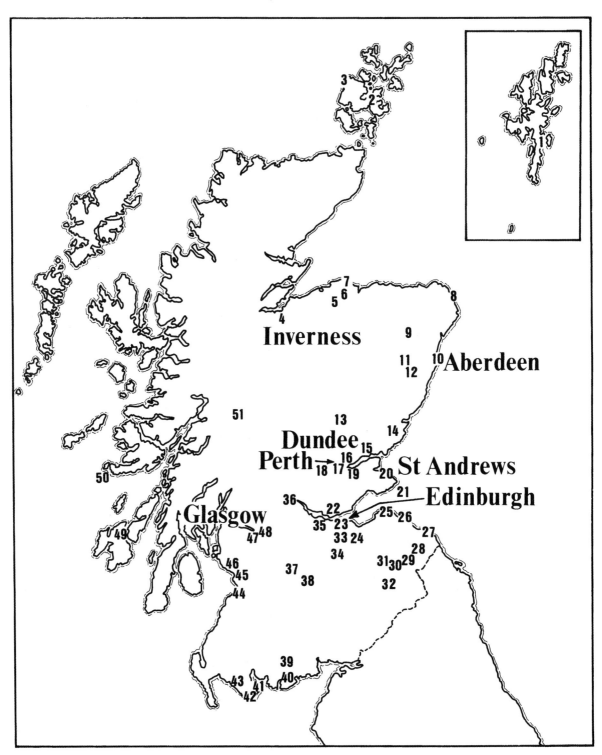

1 *Map of Scotland with principal places mentioned in the text. Ayr 44; Barhobble 43; Birsay 3; Cockpen 24; Cruggleton 41; Dunbar 25; Dundonald 45; Dundrennan 40; Dunfermline 22; Elcho 19; Elgin 6; Eyemouth 27; Finlaggan 49; The Hirsel 28; Inchaffray 18; Iona 50; Isle of May 21; Jedburgh 32; Kebister 1; Kelso 29; Kinnaird 16; Kirkwall 2; Lesmahagow 37; Linlithgow 35; Lumphanan 11; Lunan Valley 14; North Berwick 26; Paisley 47; Peebles 34; Pluscarden 5; Portencross 46; Rannoch 51; Rattray 8; Roberton 38; Roxburgh 30; Smailholm 31; Soutra 33; Spittal of Glenshee 13; Spynie 7; Stirling 36; Strachan 12; Threave 39; Wardhouse 9; Whithorn 42 (Historic Scotland).*

Introduction: it's about time…

History is but a myth which has been agreed upon. (Voltaire)

What I have set out to achieve in this book is to present a review of the results of the large number of excavations on medieval sites which have taken place during the last twenty or so years (1). This has been a time when new strategies were applied to medieval archaeology, including the rise of urban 'rescue' archaeology, which fascinated the public and sparked a greater interest in the lives of ordinary medieval people. This coincided with the first modern large-scale excavations of high-status sites like castles and abbeys, resulting in a radical reappraisal of how these places developed and functioned. Historic Scotland funded these excavations, to aid the display and interpretation of their monuments.

The term 'medieval' is loosely applied here to the period from the reign of Malcolm Canmore, in the later eleventh century, up to the Reformation of 1560. This is very much an archaeological perspective, but with reference to the wider historical context. This is not an attempt to rewrite Scottish history, but rather to take a worm's-eye view of the experience of medieval life as can only be revealed by archaeology. The very nature of the historical sources tells us little about the lives of ordinary people, and so what is attempted for the first time in these pages is a synthesis of the data produced from hundreds of excavations, where the results have provided insights into the personal experience of everyday life. The skilled archaeologist is uniquely able to do this, although the most fascinating insights occur when the archaeological and historical evidence coalesce, for example in providing the name of a tanner living in a street in Aberdeen in the early fourteenth century, whose tanning pits were found during an excavation. The two forms of evidence rarely come together, however, and are sometimes contradictory, as highlighted here, where a significantly different interpretation of the medieval economy is proposed, at odds with that garnered from the study of medieval documents.

The archaeologist reverses the process of time by stripping away the years, the events, the buildings, in an increasingly sophisticated manner. It is no accident that the proliferation of digs coincided with the refinement of analytical techniques, especially in the field of environmental archaeology. Samples are taken from pits and drains, and from floor surfaces, with informed questions being applied, and most of the answers being sought using a microscope in the laboratory after the excavation is finished. This has enabled us to understand so much more about the way that medieval people adapted to and exploited their environment, especially in and around towns. And this is important, because we now inhabit the same landscapes and townscapes which were created and altered by these people.

Not only can archaeology contribute to our

11

understanding of the inherited character of place, but it also contributes to our understanding of the origins of national culture and identity. These are the centuries when the Scotland we know today began to take shape, with improvements in agricultural production, the creation of towns and the establishment of an industrial base. But what is possibly more important than any contribution to the big picture, is what the excavations described here can offer in terms of the experience of everyday life. Here we have a unique opportunity; by knowing more of their buildings, homes, food, tools, work, personal belongings and faith, we can engage with the consciousness of our medieval ancestors, and somehow understand ourselves better; after all, these were people like us.

CHAPTER ONE

Abbeys and priories

Introduction

It has been said that the investigation of monasteries will tell us little about life in medieval Scotland, particularly as such a relatively small proportion of the population lived or worked in them. That is true to some extent in that monasteries were high-status complexes, indeed they were some of the most sophisticated and largest stone structures in the land. And yet the converse is also true in that the monasteries made a great impact on life in Scotland, beginning in 1070 when Margaret, the saintly wife of King Malcolm Canmore, invited the Benedictines to Dunfermline. Scotland was participating in a far-reaching monastic revival which affected most of Europe. This led to the formation of new monastic orders, the aims of which were simplicity and austerity. The orders were made up of canons or monks. Canons were often priests who lived in common, serving in their own church or in parish churches, while monks lived a more enclosed life. The Rule of St Benedict came to be universally accepted by monks, as that of St Augustine was by canons. From then on the crown and nobility attached great importance to, and invested enormous sums in, sustaining the monastic orders.

The influence of the monasteries was far-reaching; much of the peasantry lived on monastic estates and paid rents or dues, usually in produce, to support them. Many more worshipped in and maintained parish churches which were held by monasteries, and the income from these was destined for the parent house. In some cases the priest was provided by the monastery. With all their interests in agricultural rents, properties and estates it is not surprising that the monks endeavoured to maximize income by introducing improved systems of land management and farming. The monastic farms were called granges; these are discussed further in the context of rural settlement archaeology (see Chapter 8).

A number of themes has emerged from the results of the last twenty years of excavating monasteries. In every case there is a variety of common features which influenced site selection, the most significant being a pre-existing church. This heritage of sanctity was attractive to some of the orders, and could be of great practical help, in that they could celebrate Mass in the old church during the lengthy primary building campaign. On the Isle of May it was partly the existence of the shrine of a saint which prompted David I (1124–53) to endow the monastery, the prime purpose of which was to celebrate divine service for the repose of his own soul and those of the royal dynasty (2).

Other influencing factors were more practical, especially the availability of a water supply, of building stone and proximity to good agricultural land. The focus of

investigations has only rarely shifted away from the monastic core of church and cloister to include the rest of the immediate precinct where various essential buildings were located. The opportunities presented by environmental archaeology have increased our understanding of diet, crops and medicines, as well as the general appearance of the environment in and around monasteries.

Different orders had different requirements, a good example being the austere Cistercians' need to be withdrawn from areas of human habitation. In excavating monasteries it has not yet been possible to relate specifically the peculiarities of an order to their buildings. The Cluniacs were meant to be especially spiritual; the Augustinians were more outward-looking, often developing sites close to royal castles and offering the crown their administrative skills; whereas the Tironensians attached a great importance to manual work and thus attracted craftsmen to their order. Some were not involved in large-scale farming, and so depended more on their income from rents, tithes, fishing rights and mills, like the Valliscaulians at Pluscarden.

It is also important to bear in mind that all the monks had specific duties – chamberlain, cook, porter, gardener, provisioner, baker, guestmaster and so on – either at home or in distant properties, in addition to their devotional duties in the convent's church. Evidence for these roles can be sought in the excavations.

The evidence from excavations confirms that building work went on throughout the lives of the monasteries, with parts of each cloister incomplete, surrounded by piles of stones and roofing materials, either abandoned or awaiting use. Temporary structures were in use at various times, requiring the monasteries

2 *St Adrian's Priory, Isle of May.*

to obtain supplies of wood and thatch, and also canvas for awnings. The hemp plant, from which canvas was made, is a common find in samples taken from excavated pits and drains. The building campaigns can be seen as true expressions of the very special kind of faith which existed in medieval times; from lowliest labourer to the abbot himself, none could expect to see completion in their lifetime, but they were confident that others would. The all-pervading nature of religion in society is better understood as a result of monastic archaeology, revealing the evidence of politics with piety, of commerce and community.

Pre-monastic and colonization structures

The monastic communities of the Celtic Church were known as Culdees, and these may have been supplanted by the incoming reformed orders on a number of sites, or, as is more likely the case, to have coexisted, as happened at St Mary's Kirkheugh, St Andrews. Discoveries made during the excavations at Jedburgh, coupled with the assemblage of Saxon sculpted stones from the site, indicate the presence of a Saxon minster church. The construction of the Augustinian abbey, which began c. 1138, disturbed a cemetery and other structural remains. The minster may have stood to the north of the abbey church, and may have continued in use while the latter was being built.

The adaptability of the canons seems to have made them well suited to taking over such sites, a third case being Inchaffray in Strathearn. The evidence is less substantial here, but includes a fragment of a silver cover for an early Christian handbell, probably associated with a saint. Excavation of the north wall of the church revealed that this had been built over the remains of a 3m (10ft) wide earth bank, which may have formed part of an earlier monastic enclosure.

The intensive excavation programme at Whithorn in the far south-west has discovered many phases of settlement, which grew around the church and shrine of St Ninian. The excavations were just to the south-west of the cathedral priory founded by the austere Premonstratensian canons *c.* 1170. At the time of this colonization the excavated area contained a number of wooden houses, each about 5m (17ft) long with a central hearth, laid out in a regular pattern along streets. One of the streets ran up to the crown of the hill to the west of the new priory, where fragments of locally produced stone crosses have been found. The people living here were making jewellery and bone combs, and were Scandinavian in origin. This settlement can be interpreted as the home of a residual, monastic Hiberno-Norse population, forming part of a minster. These houses seem to be 'cells', inhabited by secular clergy who were allowed to marry, no doubt frowned on by the canons, who may have had to accept them as their neighbours well into the thirteenth century.

We know that the Cistercians and probably other orders required a considerable degree of site preparation before they would take up occupancy. Buildings to be prepared for them included a chapel, a refectory, a dormitory and a guest-house 'so that the monks may immediately serve God and live in religious discipline'. Only excavation can reveal whether this ideal was ever the reality. This phase would also have been used to secure the political and financial base for the convent before embarking on an ambitious construction programme. At Jedburgh two phases of substantial twelfth-century timber buildings were found on the river frontage under the south-west corner of the cloister. Could these have been built to the order of David I to await the arrival of the brethren?

Fragmentary colonization structures have been found at the Tironensian houses at Kelso and Lesmahagow. At Kelso, stone and timber structures of mid-twelfth-century date were found under the infirmary, along with spreads of stone chippings. This was interpreted as a mason's lodge, where the builders lived and worked. An enormous pit, 7.2m (23ft) long, was also found here, which was probably a gravel quarry. The pit contained large numbers of discarded pots thrown in when the pit was back-filled late in the twelfth century while the infirmary was being built. These pots could have been products of their own kilns, bearing in mind the emphasis placed on crafts by the Tironensians.

At Inchaffray the colonizing phase was characterized by the preparation of terraces for the main ranges and the dumping of large quantities of midden, spanning a period of as much as fifty years from the time of foundation *c.* 1200. The remains of an early kitchen with an oven were found beneath what became the west range.

Siting and water supply

Other factors which governed site selection included: suitable topography, availability of timber and building stone, and streams for powering mills and flushing drains. Sometimes political and economic factors outweighed these, as at Jedburgh where a constrained waterfront site on a steep slope was chosen because of its proximity to the royal castle and minster. And yet the monks and their masons could transcend this difficult site with a combination of hillside terracing and land-reclamation (**3**).

At Jedburgh and elsewhere it was easier to utilize streams and springs than to pump water up from the river. The excavations produced evidence for this in drains which contained lead-enriched residues and pollen derived from open countryside, indicating that the drinking water flowed from outside in lead pipes. At Lesmahagow lead piping with a T-junction was found carrying the water supply

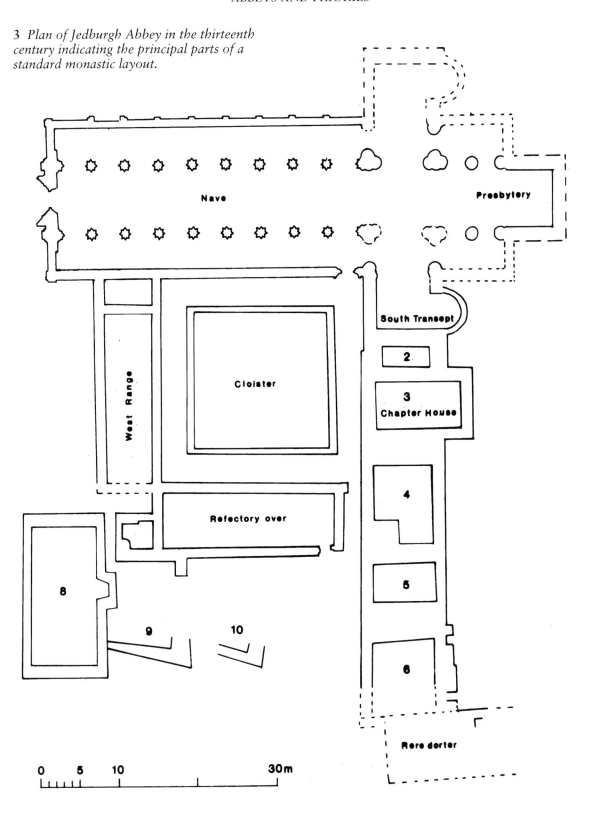

3 *Plan of Jedburgh Abbey in the thirteenth century indicating the principal parts of a standard monastic layout.*

Nave

Presbytery

South Transept

2

3
Chapter House

4

5

6

West Range

Cloister

Refectory over

8

9

10

Rere dorter

0   5   10   30m

to the west range and to the refectory kitchen. Here, and at the Cluniac priory on the May, a wash-basin (*lavatorium*) was found in precisely the same location in the cloister at the south end of the west range. The purpose of this was for hand washing before entering the dining-hall, and at the May this was fed with rain-water from the roof. At Lesmahagow the sink was provided with a drain which ran into a sump in the corner of the cloister garth (central garden) nearby. Excavations on all monastic sites encounter complex systems of drains. These are mostly simple stone-lined and capped structures of no great size.

Monastic churches

As the spiritual heart we must look to the churches to comprehend the overall development and fortunes of the religious houses. These are rarely available for excavation, one reason being that they have continued in use, sometimes as parish churches or else in ruins as family burial places. Excavations alone can provide some of the detail of appearance, such as window-glass and flooring, sadly lacking due to destruction at the Reformation.

Over 265 fragments of plain and coloured window-glass were found in the church at Elcho (Perth), in association with lead glazing bars, indicating that it was well lit. An oil lamp which hung from chains was found at Elcho, a reminder that candles and lamps were needed during the night offices and in the winter months. Burials were discovered under the floors of the church and the north cloister alley. Two main phases of church construction were recorded, resulting in a simple aisleless structure, 8m (27ft) wide by 21m (70ft) long, heavily buttressed on the south side. The east range of the cloister seems to have projected out beyond the east end of the church, as also seen at the May (**colour plate 1**).

The boggy location of Inchaffray (Perth) dictated that the builders had to provide level terraces with substantial foundation trenches packed with rubble. Fragments of the north and south walls of the nave were excavated, along with parts of a transept and sacristy, located close together on the north side of the east end. The transept was built with a massively thick north wall 2.6m ($8\frac{1}{2}$ft) wide, pierced by a doorway with two steps. This may have given access to a stair tower. A burial was found against the inside of this wall, in a location which would have allowed the wall above to contain a sculpted tomb effigy. One of the prime reasons for the endowment of the foundation was to provide a suitable burial place for the earls of Strathearn and their family.

The cloister

Latrines are always of great interest to archaeologists, because of what people dropped down them! This has certainly been true at Dundrennan Abbey (Kirkcudbright), a Cistercian house founded in the middle of the twelfth century. Excavations at the south-east corner of the cloister have investigated the latrine drain, together with a group of three rooms: interpreted as the warming-room, the novices' day room, and the reredorter undercroft, going from west to east. It might have taken some fifty years to complete the heavily buttressed reredorter, which had to be built on an artificial terrace, adjacent to the monks' dormitory. The south end was a double wall, within the thickness of which were the latrine slots which fed into a great drain running from west to east. The north wall had two windows and a doorway which gave access to the outside of the cloister. The western wall was pierced by a large, beautifully moulded doorway with steps opening into the day room. The undercroft contained many fragments of collapsed rib vaulting, which had originally supported the latrine room above on three bays. The inside wall-faces were of rough rubble, but were likely to have been plastered and painted, as was usually the case. This fine undercroft must have been an office, hence the windows, rather than simply a store (**4**).

Major alterations took place in the later fifteenth century, partially caused by subsidence at this corner. The great drain was covered to the west, probably because it had not been kept clean, and the vertical latrine channels were partially blocked to provide more support for the collapsing wall. These were replaced by smaller individual slots, more akin to secular domestic facilities, suggesting a general reduction in use and occupancy. Further evidence for a move away from communal living was found in the warming-room which was subdivided at this time into a number of rooms. The provision of two new garderobes above suggests that comfortable, private accommodation existed there for guests or senior officials. The great drain had been allowed to silt up completely by the mid-sixteenth century.

Lesmahagow was established as a daughter house of Kelso in the middle of the twelfth century, on a site with a pre-existing church. It was standard in all monasteries to have a roofed, open-sided walkway, about 2m (6½ft) wide – running around the cloister buildings. Burials were found under the east alley walk, which is often the case, especially in the vicinity of the entrance to the chapter house. The central cloister garth was examined, and found to be composed of finely tilled soil, indicating that this had always been a garden.

The dining-hall (refectory) was located in the south range; originally this was built with an entrance from the cloister in the north wall, and was 3m (10ft) longer to the west, where it butted right up against the west range. The kitchen may have been at this end, serving a single-storey dining-hall, with an open trussed roof. The priory was badly damaged by the English in 1335 and following this the refectory was remodelled: the north door was blocked and the west end was turned into a passageway giving access from the cloister alley into both the refectory and the outer court to the south. Another major change followed about 150 years later when the south wall was completely rebuilt, and the north wall had the springing for a vault added to create a vaulted cellar, with the dining-hall now at first-floor level. This was a more elaborate arrangement although the quality of the masonry was inferior to the good Romanesque ashlar blocks used in the primary work. Again, as noted elsewhere, the excavations revealed that by the mid-sixteenth century the structures were neglected and decaying, with evidence of squatter occupation. The exception is the west range, which having often contained the private accommodation for abbot or prior was ideally suited for conversion to secular lodgings.

The precinct

The church and cloister occupied only a small part of an enclosed block of land known as the precinct. This is where the other buildings were located necessary for the essential day-to-day running of the monastery. Investigation of these structures will help us understand how the religious houses functioned: here were the infirmaries, almshouses, barns and storehouses, gardens and orchards, workshops, forges and kilns, mills, stables, chapels and graveyards.

Precinct bounds were marked by water courses and by banks and ditches, and eventually by walls. Some walls were provided with defensive towers, as can be seen surviving at St Andrews. So these boundaries could be defensive, but were primarily to keep the monks in their sacred space physically separate from the sinners beyond. They enclosed large areas, as at Dunfermline where, right up to the sixteenth century, the precinct was larger than the area of the adjoining burgh. Recent excavations at the south-east corner of this precinct straddled the boundary, giving a rare opportunity to contrast activities on both

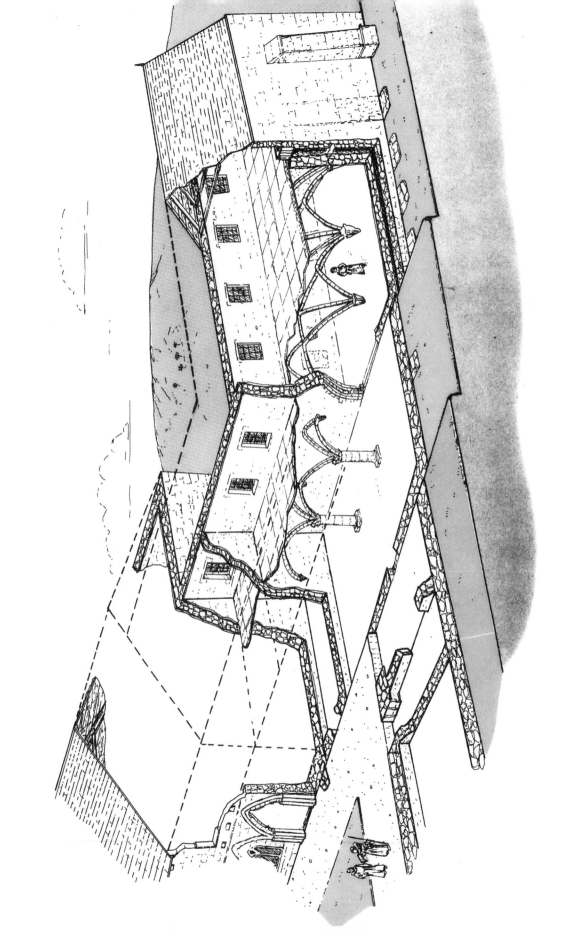

sides. It was found that a stream was artificially enlarged in the twelfth century to create the boundary, no doubt augmented by an internal bank. This was formalized in the fourteenth century when the lengthy process of building the precinct wall finally reached this remote corner.

To the north of the abbey church in Dunfermline, not far from the shrine of St Margaret, stands the Abbot House, which has long been thought to have originated as a defended town house of the later sixteenth century (see **45**). Investigations above and below ground have revealed that this was in fact the abbot's lodging, built up against the precinct wall in the middle of the fifteenth century. This house had at least two storeys, and on the first floor a beautiful traceried window was discovered, hidden away behind centuries of alterations. From this window the abbot could keep an eye on his commercial interests in the town below, while still being within the sacred precinct. The back garden was created at the same time as the house, but for 150 years before had been part of the extensive graveyard on the north side of the church.

Inchaffray was built on an artificial island in the marshy flood-plain of the Pow Water, Strathearn (Perthshire). Parts of the precinct wall were revealed by excavation and geophysical survey; the wall was found close to the south-west corner of the cloister where it was of massive construction. Here it was dated to the late thirteenth century, and clearly intended for defence against incursions by man and by the Pow flood. The geophysical survey picked up this wall again, over 40m (133ft) west of the cloister, and also detected a large building, to the north-west of the church. This measured 36m (120ft) by 18m (60ft), and

could well be the Great Barn, possibly built after reclamation works extended the precinct island to the west. The monks were certainly capable of carrying out such large-scale engineering works, and may well have canalized the Pow, as there is a reference dated 1489 to the 'digging of a canal for little ships'.

We have seen that regular episodes of purposeful destruction are a common feature of the archaeological record of most monasteries. The aftermath of one such event, the sacking of Pluscarden Priory in 1390, was graphically revealed when a large pit was discovered during excavations close to the west end of the church. This stone-lined pit had originally been constructed for cool storage, possibly of dairy produce. Laboratory analysis of the contents has shown, however, that it later became a latrine. The pit contained a fist-sized organic deposit which was largely made up of remnants of worn-out clothing which had been used for 'sanitary purposes'. The finds dated the infill to the fourteenth century. Parasite remains, which had originated in the human gut, helped to identify much of the contents as faecal material. The insect remains were also very interesting and helpful; they were mainly dark-loving species, and this coupled with other evidence suggest that the cesspit was covered with a trapdoor to the east, nearest the church. The finds included fragments of coloured window-glass from the damaged church, and butchered cat and dog carcasses. The pollen in the pit was mainly cereals, probably ingested from poor barley broth. And so a picture emerges of monastic life in disarray, with the cloister and proper latrines in ruins, and the dietary evidence pointing to a time of hunger.

The infirmary was where the sick were treated, and where the old and infirm of the community would live. The monks were fond of being bled, and would have this done in the infirmary on a regular basis, which was supposedly the only time they were allowed a diet rich in meat. The excavated infirmary hall

4 Reconstruction of the reredorter undercroft at Dundrennan Abbey.

at Kelso Abbey was 16m (53ft) wide and probably 32m (106ft) long. This was a stone building which had replaced the primary timber hall in the thirteenth century. Two parallel rows of pillar bases, alternating circular and octagonal in design, ran along the building to create two side aisles or wards for the sick. This building may also have housed a chapel, and close at hand might have been a kitchen and a house for distributing alms. By the early fifteenth century the excavations revealed that the hall was in a decayed state and was remodelled by being subdivided into individual free-standing cells. Each cell was provided with a fireplace, chimney-stack, partition walls and paving, placing greater emphasis on the comfort of the individual and taking the brethren further away from the ideals of communal piety and asceticism.

Jedburgh Abbey

Jedburgh was founded close to major centres of power in what must have seemed an ideal location until events took a turn for the worse: the abbey was attacked and damaged in 1305, 1410, 1416, 1464, 1523 and 1544–5. Repair programmes followed each attack but the last. The abbey stood in a large precinct, bounded to the south and east by the Jed Water, which powered the mill and flushed the reredorter 80m (264ft) south of the church. The burgh grew up around the abbey to the north, encouraged by the economic opportunities created by a great monastery and a royal castle (**colour plate 2**).

Some of the most interesting results relate to the primary colonization and development of the site, including a gruesome discovery in a twelfth-century sewer trench, just outside the east range (5). A human torso was found in the trench, along with a group of objects, including a walrus ivory comb (see back cover), a seal or pendant, a horn buckle and a whetstone, which had belonged to a person of

5 *Excavation of the east range of Jedburgh Abbey, with the twelfth-century sewer trench (centre foreground).*

wealth and rank. This seems to have been a bungled robbery, with the victim being killed and his dismembered body, along with some of the loot, disposed of in the confusion and activity of a building site. The ditch was back-filled soon after, an event dated by a coin of Henry II to *c.* 1170. By this time work was certainly underway on the church and possibly the chapter house, but probably not on the rest of the east range. The environmental evidence identified the function of the trench from the presence of human gut parasites, along with abundant pollen of the plant tormentil. The latter has astringent properties and was used as a remedy for diarrhoea. A high concentration of metallic lead showed that the trench was flushed by the piped water supply down into the river.

The excavations have shown that it took one hundred years to complete the east range, beginning adjacent to the abbey church and ending with the reredorter. The south end of the east range was built into unstable river-bank material; the rooms here were therefore found to have been massively built and vaulted to support the oversailing dormitory floor above. This included a room at the lowest point of the cloister, at the south-east corner, which had walls 3.5m (11$\frac{1}{2}$ ft) thick supporting a quadripartite vaulted ceiling, more than 3m (10ft) in height. This primary thirteenth-century work was of very tightly jointed ashlar, with no windows. This room may have been a food store, which would usually have been a function of the west range. But the primary west range was found to have been small, and so it is possible to imagine food supplies being unloaded through the east door of this room which gave access to the precinct beyond. A door in the west wall would have opened on to a passageway which led up a flight of stairs to the cloister. The reredorter was located to the south of this undercroft, and the small part available for excavation was found to be of the same high-quality ashlar.

Following the ravages of the fourteenth century, the undercroft to the north of the reredorter was rebuilt as the base for a large, free-standing house. The north half of the cellar was abandoned, however, and used as a midden, which is likely to have been dumped while this area was unoccupied during a period of rebuilding. This kitchen waste provided much information about diet, particularly the fact that the traditional meat-less diet had been abandoned and instead large amounts of butchered joints were being con-sumed. Beef and lamb were preferred to pork and wild (hunted) species, and sea-fish was also popular. At Jedburgh there is every indication that by the later fourteenth century the move towards greater comfort was well underway, with a number of kitchens around the cloister catering for individual abbey officials in their lodgings.

The excavations revealed a fascinating and unique building sequence at the south-west corner of the cloister. Here the difficulties of the riverbank site had to be overcome, following the completion of the east range, to allow the construction of what may initially have been a guest range. The difficult site was conquered by an ingenious design: a wooden building raft was discovered, made of massive oak beams, dated by dendrochronology (tree-ring dating) to c. 1260. The south wall of the house was built on this foundation, and probably stood to a height of 20m (66ft) with a roof-line level with that of the refectory. The house contained an internal covered pend which enabled access along the riverbank without entering the house. Drains and garde-robes emptied into the river here, and kitchen waste would also have been dumped, so elaborate steps were taken in the design to ensure that the river hit the wall forcefully enough to stop stagnant pools from forming. Another two building platforms were con-structed on the riverbank to the east of this range, both with acutely angled south-east corners, designed to deflect the flow to flush the reredorter drain. The platform to the east of the range was not built on, but was probably a yard with a jetty, where supplies were delivered for the main kitchen, just 10m (33ft) to the north, and also giving the abbot and visitors access to the river (6, 7).

The guest range was an elaborate structure with a vaulted cellar equipped with a large fireplace, and domestic accommodation above allowing direct access out at cloister alley level. It would have presented a grand face to the west towards the abbey gatehouse and to the royal castle.

Much of the second building campaign may have taken place during the stability of the latter part of the reign of David II (1329–71), and before the destruction of Jedburgh Castle

by the Scots in 1409. During and after this campaign the canons looked to improve the defences of the abbey, especially to the north and west which lacked the natural defences of the river. Towers were added to the precinct wall along the Castlegate and the Canongate. The excavations threw up considerable data concerning the structural decay and constriction of use of the cloister in the fifteenth century.

The great cloister itself seems to have been adapted to military use during one or more of the military occupations of Jedburgh in the mid-sixteenth century. The excavation results indicated that the already ruinous abbot's house, and parts of the east range, were converted into makeshift artillery platforms, linked by a rampart to the towers on the precinct wall and in the town. Guns may also have been mounted on the church tower, effectively bringing to an end the proper functioning of this great Augustinian monastery.

St Adrian's Priory, Isle of May

This was a small Benedictine priory founded in the 1140s by David I, as a daughter house of Reading Abbey, on the site of the shrine of a local saint and his followers, who were reputedly martyred by the Vikings in 875 (8). There may never have been more than about ten monks here along with a few servants. Ownership of the monastery and its extensive lands was contested between Reading and St Andrews during the Wars of Independence. St Andrews took possession early on in the fourteenth century, resulting in the site being

8 *East range and chapter house of St Adrian's Priory (foreground), with church and cemetery beyond.*

effectively abandoned in favour of a new monastery built on their lands in Pittenweem, only a few miles from the May. The documents record raids around the time of abandonment, which are likely to have resulted in the church and other buildings being seriously damaged. During more peaceful times, the May reached prominence as a place of pilgrimage, and not surprisingly the canons of Pittenweem kept a single member of their convent on the island to maintain the shrine, to give hospitality to pilgrims and to receive their money!

There are many important reasons why this site was selected for excavation: because of the possibility of discovering rare remains of an early Christian monastery on the east coast;

6 *Jedburgh Abbey excavations; the line of the medieval river frontage and pend under the guest range can be seen (left).*

7 *Reconstruction of Jedburgh Abbey as it would have looked in the later thirteenth century.*

because of the opportunity to pursue the archaeology of pilgrimage; because the twelfth-century cloister and church are likely to be well preserved in this isolated location; and because of the unusual early date of abandonment. The entire island formed the precinct and would have been exploited by the monks, and so a study is also being made of their impact on the environment.

Other environmental analysis indicates that cereals could never have been cultivated, and that the island could support only about fifty sheep and a few cattle. The excavations have shown that sea-birds and seals were consumed, along with large quantities of fish paid as a teind (tenth) of every catch from the boats which harvested the renowned fisheries around the May, and used the monks' harbour. Otherwise they were wholly dependent on supplies from their estates, and on trading fish for other foodstuff at local markets.

The excavations have exposed a standard claustral plan with the church on the north and three other ranges around an open garth (9). The church was 14m (46ft) in length, with a simple rectangular plan. The only surviving entrance was in the west wall, found complete with jambs and threshold. None of the original floor survived; different parts of this would have been covered in stone slabs, while the east end around the high altar and the shrine of the saint would have been tiled with ceramic floor-tiles, some of which may have been decorated. The church roof was clad with stone tiles, imported from a quarry near Dundee. Ceramic green-glazed tiles were used on other buildings. All of these materials have been found in great quantities in the destruction deposits which date back to the fourteenth century.

The church was built against the east range, indicating that the monks worshipped in a pre-existing chapel while the primary building works went ahead. The east range contained pillar bases which had helped support the dormitory on the floor above (10). The refectory was on the first floor of the south range, and the excavations have so far uncovered drains and floor surfaces from the ground-

9 *St Adrian's Priory; reconstruction of the monastery completed c. 1250.*

10 *Pillar bases in the chapter house of St Adrian's Priory, surrounded by demolition debris from the fourteenth-century raids.*

floor cellars and kitchen. The west range was converted into secular use in the mid-sixteenth century retaining much of the original structure. This probably survived so well because it had become a guest range for pilgrims and accommodation for the hermit from the fourteenth century on. While the church was in ruins the shrine and relics of the saint were moved into a vaulted chapel at the north end of this building, to be visited by thousands of pilgrims, including James IV who came on a number of occasions.

One of the aims of the project was to find where the monks and pilgrims were buried, and by examining the skeletons to discover more about how these people lived and died. The area to the north of the church was investigated by trial trenching and by geophysical survey. Sure enough a burial ground was found here but not with the expected medieval form of graves. Layers of burials were found, separated by layers of beach stones (11). This raises the question: why bury a Christian population under a burial cairn, a pagan form of burial, when there were other areas nearby where graves could be dug? Maybe this was the preferred burial place for monks and latterly for pilgrims, originating as the sepulchre for Adrian and the other martyrs of the ninth-century massacre.

One burial here has helped to illuminate contemporary belief and the motivation behind pilgrimage. At some time in the fifteenth century, a young man was buried at

11 *Monks and pilgrims under the burial cairn at St Adrian's Priory.*

the east end of the ruined church. What was so extraordinary about this was that he had been buried with a scallop shell in his mouth (**12**). The scallop is the symbol of St James the Great, whose burial place at Santiago de Compostela was (and still is) the most popular pilgrimage place outside of Rome and the Holy Land. St James was the patron of the Stewart dynasty and was popular with many Scots, some of whom are known to have embarked upon this pilgrimage. Could the young man buried on the May be a Santiago pilgrim, who had made that arduous journey from Fife to north-west Spain and then, when he died, was laid to rest with the badge of St James in his mouth, so that when he arose on the Last Day he could clearly be identified as one of the blessed? Other burials associated

with scallop shells have been found, including one other from Scotland found in excavations at the Hirsel medieval church, and others found in England and on the Continent, but never with the shell in the mouth of the deceased. A pierced and painted scallop badge, which had been attached to clothing, was found during the excavations on the High Street in Perth.

The emerging story of the robbing and reuse of the monastery buildings is of great interest. Much of the tiles and good building stone would have been reused when the west range was converted into a house in the sixteenth century. We know that the shell of the church was sufficiently intact at this time to allow a two-roomed workshop to be built against the north and west walls. An iron furnace was found in the west room, with a large stone sink originally from the monks' kitchen being used as a quenching trough.

The great drain of Paisley Abbey

The discovery and investigation of the Paisley Abbey drain has been doubly amazing; not only have we had a glimpse of an intact piece of high-quality monastic architecture, hidden for hundreds of years, but also we have gained a rare insight into the richness and diversity of the cultural life of medieval Scotland, from the wealth of finds sealed in the drain.

Paisley was a large and wealthy monastery founded by the Stewarts *c.* 1163. Major building works were required in the fourteenth century following the usual damage caused by the wars with the English in the first half of the century. The great drain was constructed as part of this programme, transforming an existing open drain. The varied nature and quality of the architecture shows that the drain was built in stages, some of the finest rib-vaulted sections being the first to be completed (**13**). Little is known about the layout of the precinct at Paisley, and knowing the line of the

12 *Scallop shell burial at St Adrian's Priory.*

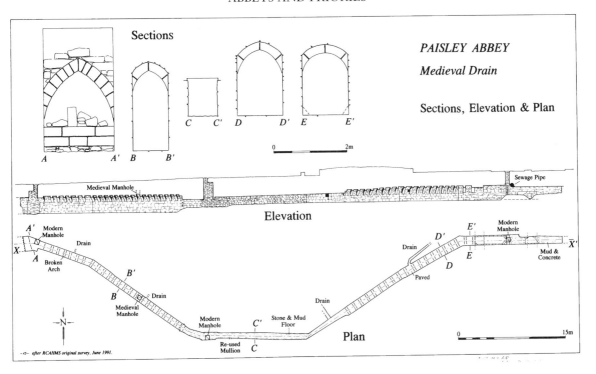

PAISLEY ABBEY

Medieval Drain

Sections, Elevation & Plan

13 *Paisley Abbey drain.*

14 *Fifteenth-century monks' chamber-pot from the Paisley Abbey drain.*

drain will help locate some of the other major structures such as the reredorter, kitchens and infirmary, which would have been served by the drain (**colour plate 3**).

The drain is blocked in places which has helped preserve silts which were laid down during the fifteenth century, when the fabric of the abbey was documented as being in decay, and when the drain was not being regularly flushed out. Limited excavations have produced the best assemblage of medieval artefacts and ecofacts ever found in the west of Scotland. The pottery included a complete chamber-pot (**14**), which might have been dropped one morning while being emptied down a latrine by a sleepy monk! This group of material showed a marked contrast between the poor-quality local wares and those imported from Germany and the Low Countries. Further evidence for trade with these countries and with London was found in the form of 16 lead seals, which came to the abbey attached to bolts of cloth. One of these was from Valenciennes, which was famed at

the time for the production of high-quality dyed linen. But why did the monks have so much cloth? The most likely explanation is that the abbey was involved in the cloth trade for profit, or that they obtained these goods in exchange for wool and hides from their estates.

Recreational activities were represented by dice and gaming pieces, along with a tuning peg from a stringed instrument. Music was an important part of monastic life, and remarkably the drain has produced fragments of musical notation, inscribed on two slates (**15**). They are both short passages of polyphonic (choral) composition, identical in style and dated to the mid-fifteenth century. They were permanent copies which may have been used for training choristers. The liberal arts are also represented by the discovery of a further slate inscribed with secular love lyrics; a unique discovery from a Scottish monastic context. The slate was inscribed on both sides by two different people, with errors being corrected by scraping away the surface.

The richness of the artefacts has been matched by the palaeoenvironmental assemblage preserved and forgotten for centuries in the waterlogged silts: wood, bone, shells, seeds, textile and plant remains were all present. These tiny fragments, recovered by controlled sampling and sieving and identified in the laboratory, can now help us to understand more about food, medicine and the environment. More than 140 different plants were recognized, only a small proportion of which were grown or used by the monks. Most were blown in from the nearby riverbank and surrounding fields, and when examined as a group all help to reconstruct the abbey environs.

15 *Slate inscribed with choral music from the Paisley Abbey drain.*

Some of the plants found in the drain were imported to Scotland by monks to grow in their physic gardens, and had specific medicinal uses recorded in medieval pharmacological textbooks known as herbals. Examples from the drain include: great celandine which was used as eye ointment, and caper spurge which was a purgative. The drain also produced hemlock and white opium poppy, taken internally as anaesthetic or externally as a pain killer, both of which could be dangerous if wrongly used. Bog mosses were found which are known to have been combined with antiseptic plants as an absorbent wound dressing. Mosses were also used as toilet paper.

Cereals from the abbey estates were found: wheat was used to make flour for the monks' bread, and barley was used to make ale, the staple drink. The animal bones showed that the monks were eating joints of beef, pork, and lamb or kid. Nutmeg and ginger were found which were expensive spices imported from the East Indies; strong spices were needed to disguise the flavour of bad or preserved meat. Another costly import found in the drain were figs imported from the Mediterranean; these are a fairly common find from cesspits as they were taken as a purgative. Apples, brambles, raspberries, bilberries, rowans and hazelnuts were all identified. Another important part of this varied diet was fish, both sea and freshwater.

Soutra Hospital

The lengthy research project at Soutra in the Borders has opened a window onto the world of medieval medicine. In the middle of the twelfth century one of only three high-status hospitals in Scotland was established here by the Augustinians, on an inhospitable upland site. Soutra was on the 'King's highway', which had been the Roman road between England and Scotland. This was not a mon-astic house, and yet it is useful to consider the results in the context of monastic medicine.

We know that this hospital served many functions: to offer alms for the poor, to give hospitality to travellers, to serve as a place of legal sanctuary, and to treat the sick, including lepers, lunatics and the old. The results from Soutra make a valuable comparison with the Paisley drain which has also produced medicinal plant remains, but from an ordinary monastery where medicine was not the prime function. Soutra is thought to have had a doctor or *medicus*, as opposed to the less specialized herbalist and infirmarer of the monastic houses.

Crop marks on aerial photographs indicate that Soutra comprised an enclosed 'citadel' covering 700sq m (half a square mile) in area. The hospital seems to have stood on the main road, fronted by a substantial gatehouse. The aerial photographs and the geophysical survey results have identified a double compound. In these compounds might be found the infirmary hall, chapel, kitchen, bakehouse, courtyards, servants' accommodation and physic garden.

One of the first things that was looked for was blood; buckets of it. Bloodletting was popular in medieval times, especially with the monastic communities, and was also a basic element of lay medicine. Special tests to identify tiny quantities of blood have been successfully applied to the deposits on this impermeable clay-based site to identify where blood and therefore other infirmary waste deposits might be found. Some deposits which tested positive for blood also contained the pollen of cloves, which had to be imported all the way from East Africa. One of the special restorative treats for the 'bleeders' was wine spiced with cloves. Indeed, the site has produced evidence of a number of exotic spices, interpreted as being in a medicinal context, including: liquorice, opium poppy, pepper, ginger and nutmeg. Large sums were needed to satisfy the demand for these

31

16 *Fourteenth-century drain at Soutra Hospital between the living-quarters and the church, illustrating the deposition of medicinal waste.*

substances, some of which came from half-way around the world.

The excavations have focused on what may be the basement cellar of an accommodation block, separated from the church to the south by a drain which ran out of the complex, west under the main road (**16**). What is interpreted as a ready-to-use anaesthetic preparation was retrieved from an occupation deposit in one of the cellars. This was a combination of 574 seeds from three species of poisonous plants: black henbane, opium poppy and hemlock, in a context dated to the early fourteenth century. This matches medieval recipes for general anaesthetic to be taken before major surgery, presumably amputation.

Soutra played an important part in the Wars of Independence. Edward II and his army camped here *en route* to Bannockburn, and some features discovered during excavation have been interpreted as evidence of abuse of structures and choking of drains consistent with the presence of a large occupying force, possibly on a number of occasions. It is claimed that extremely large amounts of medical waste have been found in these contexts, notably in the drain which ran between the possible church and the structure to the north. These samples are characterized as testing positive for blood, tainted with lead originating from a piped water supply flushed down the drain. The organic content of this waste might be interpreted as: herbs and spices; fragments of linen dressings; types of pottery associated with pharmaceutical use; and items of surgeons' kit, including a possible scalpel knife blade. These have been found mixed with food waste, along with traces of quicklime, which may have been used to deodorize and disinfect dangerous deposits produced during the treatment of wounds.

The three most common microscopic plant remains found in combination at Soutra are opium poppy, hemp and flax. The first two have known narcotic properties; the latter was also used in the preparation of medieval drugs, or alternatively may have come from flax made into linen dressings.

Numerous pottery sherds found at Soutra have been tested to identify what they contained. This is not done routinely on excavations and has proved to be successful in one case at least. An ointment jar, a specialized form of vessel, was analysed and found to have contained a pain-killing preparation composed of opium poppy in a base of animal grease. Other plant remains have been ascribed a use in obstetrics. Ergot fungus and juniper berries have been found in fourteenth-century contexts, and were believed to have been used to bring on uterine contractions either in childbirth or in abortions.

Poor hygiene and bad food ensured that gut problems were a fact of life in medieval Scotland, and a reliable indicator of medical treatment for this complaint has been found at Soutra in the form of tormentil pollen. This occurred in the excavations here and at Jedburgh Abbey and elsewhere, always in association with the eggs of parasitic worms. Tormentil may have been regularly applied as a cure for worms and diarrhoea, and it has even been suggested that the monks were administering it in food on a daily basis.

The results from Soutra are important and fascinating, and yet there might be alternative interpretations for the use of some of the plant remains, other than the strictly medical interpretation which has been applied with such certainty by the excavator. It remains to be seen whether an ordinary monastery like Paisley can produce as much evidence of medicinal practice from the well-preserved and sealed deposits in the drain, as has been identified at Soutra.

CHAPTER TWO

Holy beggars

There were forty-five houses of mendicant friars in Scotland, plus eight houses of Trinitarians who lived a comparable way of life to the friars but were not mendicants. The term 'mendicant' refers to the fact that the friars were not originally allowed to own property, as part of their lives of absolute poverty, and therefore had to seek alms from the community and wealthy individuals where they lived. Not surprisingly, this presented some difficulties when they had to build churches and cloisters.

The orders were attracted to towns because here were populations large enough to support their organized begging. Here they could find patrons or burgesses who would provide them with a site and maybe even a church. There are similarities between the claustral friaries and the monasteries. There were also significant functional differences, however, which archaeology can elucidate. Unlike monks, the friars were freed of some of the ties of monastic life, allowing them to practise secular preaching, thus becoming more integrated with the local communities. They were also successful as confessors, and by providing burial space in their precincts they attracted income away from the parish churches.

The results of the excavations have shown that the friary cloisters tended to be small, with a general similarity in layout to that of the monasteries. On each excavated site long churches have been found, which is not surprising when considering the functional aspect of preaching, necessitating the provision of a sizeable nave to accommodate a large congregation. Outside the cloister a friary would have had other buildings, including a kitchen, brewhouse, bakehouse and servants' quarters. Beside these would be gardens and orchards; the friars were reputed to be great gardeners and produced the first writings on horticulture.

The Whitefriars

The Carmelite ('Whitefriars') friary in Aberdeen was founded *c*. 1270 on a site partly built on reclaimed land beside the developing harbour. The construction work was caught up in the Wars of Independence, and would have been badly affected by a battle fought in this part of Aberdeen when Edward III of England ordered a raid in 1336. Excavations have revealed the west end of the church, and parts of the west range, giving some idea of the scale and development of the friary, and fragments of coloured window-glass give hints as to the decoration of the church (**colour plates 4, 5**). The characteristically long, narrow church *c*. 35m (115ft) in length was contained within a walled precinct, the bounds of which are reflected today in the persisting medieval street pattern. A large number of burials, representing a total of around 200 individuals, were found in the small proportion of the west end of the church available for excavation. Further excavations underway at the time of writing (summer 1994) have revealed the north-west corner of the church, with many more burials both inside and out (**17**). This corner was buttressed, close to a north-west doorway of good-quality masonry.

Burials began at the end of the fourteenth century, which probably gives a good indication of the date of completion of the church, and carried on beyond the demolition of the church in 1560. A piped water system was found, which may have been supplying a kitchen in the west range, where a sizeable fireplace was uncovered. A number of simple taps known as spigots have been found, which

17 Carmelite friary, Aberdeen; buttressed north-west corner of church with doorway.

were probably used with barrels of ale or wine stored in the west range.

Whereas all four friaries in Aberdeen were accommodated within the bounds of the medieval burgh, this was not possible at Perth, presumably because the burgh had developed so intensively by the thirteenth century. The four friaries in Perth were all located outside the town walls, including the Carmelite friary founded in 1262, which was located in a suburb to the north-west, on one of the main roads out of the town (**colour plate 6**). Part of the east end of the church, the kirkyard, and the east range were excavated, revealing that, as usual, the church was the first building to be completed. By contrast with the church in Aberdeen, relatively few burials were found here within the east end. This was a prestigious location, close to the high altar where wealthier patrons and important friars might be buried. The importance of these individuals

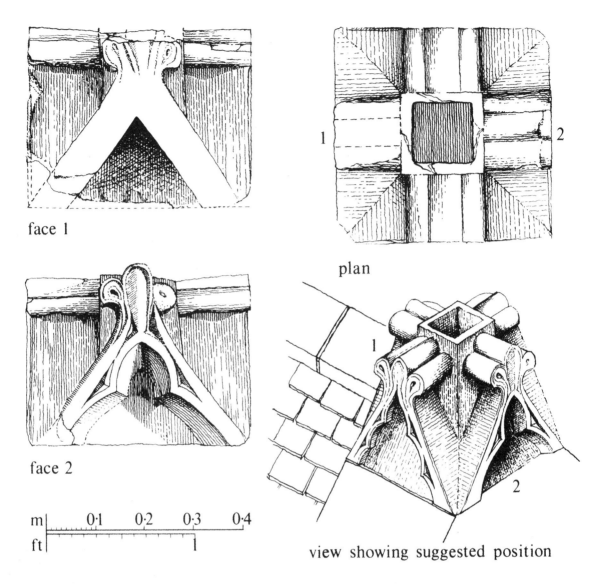

face 1

plan

face 2

m | 0·1 0·2 0·3 0·4
ft | 1

view showing suggested position

18 *Decorated stone finial from the church of the Carmelite friary, Perth.*

was reinforced by the fact that three of the eleven burials were within wooden plank-lined graves. The church was about 8m (26ft) wide, but the full length is unknown.

Although the Carmelite churches were relatively simple structures, excavations have shown that they were not without embellishment. At Perth a decorated carved-stone finial, originally from the east-end gable, was found in the demolition rubble (**18**). This could have

surmounted a niche for a holy statue. Around 1300 a further two buildings, forming part of the east range, were built up against the east end of the south wall of the church. The first of these was probably the sacristy, which was where the priest kept altar vessels and other treasures. Outside, immediately to the east, a large ditch was found which terminated against the east wall. This was too large to have simply been a drainage ditch, although being so close to the church it was unlikely to have been a sewer trench. The full length of the east range was excavated measuring 21m

(69ft) in length. This may only have been *c.* 5m (17ft) wide, with the friars' dormitory at first-floor level. The friary kirkyard was found to the east of the church, being the normal location, but again unlike Aberdeen, very few burials were found here.

The friary was demolished in May 1559 by the Perth mob, following the incendiary preaching of John Knox. The demolition debris is quite helpful in that it allows us to envisage how the standing structures looked. The buildings were of local sandstone, some roofed with stone, and some with ceramic tiles. The same quarry near Aberlemno seems to have supplied stone roof-tiles to all three of the excavated Carmelite friaries. Lots of painted window-glass were found near the east end of the church, along with plain glass and lead kames. The large ditch to the east of the sacristy seems to have been back-filled very quickly at this time, and a surprising discovery was made in the top infill. A body had been dumped here face down; could this have been a murder victim, or else a relatively fresh body exhumed from a wall tomb during the demolition of the church (**19**)? The site of

the friary church continued in use as an infrequent burial place into the seventeenth century, as was found at Aberdeen.

The Carmelite house at Linlithgow was established in 1401 on the site of an existing chapel (see p. 44), which was utilized as the nave of the priory church, adapted and extended to the east to measure 36.5m (120ft) in length. The east wall of the old chapel was reduced in height and pierced by a doorway with a wooden screen above. Just to the east of this was a narrow stone base for the choir-stalls built up against the north and south walls. The east end was divided into two equal halves by a wooden screen, isolating the presbytery to the east, which had a raised floor originally covered in stone slabs. The base of the high altar was found here, with socketed stones later added at the north-east and the south-east corners (**20**). These were supports for a wooden retable, maybe a screen and canopy, which rose up above the altar. Altar bases were found in the nave against the

19 *Body dumped face down in a ditch at the Carmelite friary, Perth.*

20 *The high altar of the Carmelite friary church, Linlithgow, with corner sockets to support a screen (in the foreground).*

base of the screen. Burials were found inside, and all around the outside of the church.

By *c.* 1430 a building was added to the west end of the church. This may have been the base of a bell-tower, or else a mortuary chapel. It was located between the church and a detached latrine 10m (33ft) from the west end of the church, which had originated as part of the pre-friary priest's house and had carried on in use. This excavation produced the only evidence from a friary of colonization-phase structures dating from the initial period of church building, before any of the cloister was built. A temporary building, which may have been a mason's lodge, or else temporary accommodation for the friars, was found to the south-east of the church, along with areas of cobbling.

The east range was built on top of graves during the second half of the fifteenth century. At the north end, immediately against the church, was a very narrow space which probably contained a night-stair, giving access from the dormitory on the first floor down into the church. The larger room to the south of this was probably the sacristy, and to the south of this again was the chapter house, which had a sprung wooden floor. A room to the south of this was probably the parlour or common room, which had a large central fireplace within the south wall. Later on in the fifteenth century the south range was built. The west end of this range and much of the west range were not excavated. The south range was divided into three rooms on the ground floor by partition walls, the refectory being the largest room in the middle, possibly with the kitchen at the west end. This range was of fairly insubstantial construction and may indicate that this was only a single-storey block. The west range would have been used for accommodating guests, for storage and for administrative offices (**21**).

The cloister alley walkways did not have arcade walls, and this area only seems to have been levelled and generally tidied-up towards the end of the fifteenth century on completion of the main building phases. A mortar mixer was found at the south-east corner, along with

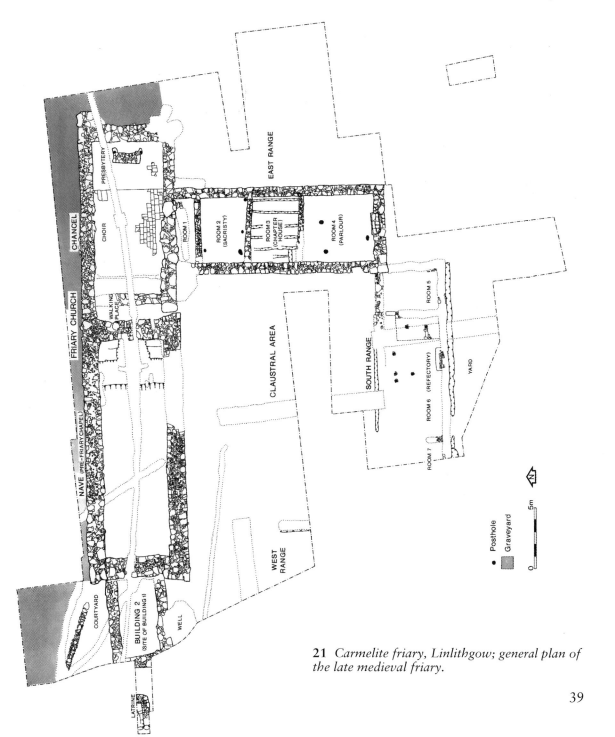

21 *Carmelite friary, Linlithgow; general plan of the late medieval friary.*

some rough areas of cobbling within the garth. A few burials were found here. The cloister garth, the open area in the middle, was probably about 20m (66ft) wide. This area was never completed, indicating a period of decay early in the sixteenth century. Although this site seems to have been systematically demolished at the Reformation, the historical evidence suggests that some of the friars were allowed to live on here after 1559, with burial space reserved for them.

At Linlithgow glass was found around all three ranges in the cloister indicating that the windows were extensively glazed. All of the coloured and decorated glass, however, was found smashed below the east and west gables of the church. Linlithgow also produced evidence of painted lime plaster giving some indication of the internal decoration of the church and other buildings. One of the most fascinating discoveries from the east range were a number of shells and fragments of pottery used for mixing pigments (**colour plate 7**). These would certainly have been used in painting decoration on to plaster, but they might also have been used by the friars in panel and manuscript painting. Some other finds were excavated on the Carmelite sites which were closely identified with the religious function of the complexes. These included the thirteenth- or fourteenth-century seal matrix from Perth (**see colour plate 6**), along with book fittings found on all three sites.

The Blackfriars

Alexander II (1214–49) was responsible for introducing the Dominican Order (the 'Blackfriars') into Scotland, enabling them to establish a house in the north-east suburbs of Perth immediately outside the town walls. This was located just to the west of the site of the royal castle which had been destroyed in the Tay floods of 1209. The Dominican friary became a focus for royal events in Perth, being a meeting-place for Parliament, and a royal residence until the murder of James I here in 1437. A contemporary description gives a very grand impression of how this friary looked, complete with separate king's lodgings with a private latrine and tennis court. Excavations here were restricted to a rather small area, and unfortunately did not uncover any of the latter.

Part of the south end of the east range was investigated, possibly including part of the reredorter. Just to the east of the buildings was a metalled road which separated the east range from the cemetery. Here the graves were well ordered with space between each one, and no apparent intercutting, which is a common feature of intensively used medieval graveyards. Two of the burials were found in coffins, the rest having been buried in simple shrouds, which was the common practice. This neat regimentation might indicate that this was the friars' own cemetery, rather than being a public one, which may have been elsewhere within the bounds of the friary.

Although in general the friars were thought to have integrated well with the secular populations, there were also ample opportunities for friction, and it is known that in the sixteenth century the Blackfriars were involved in property disputes with the burgh. They were certainly not popular at this time as witnessed by an infamous event in 1543 known as the Friars Pot incident. This records when a mob broke into the cloister and stole the friars' great cooking pot, complete with their dinner inside, which was then paraded through the streets. This illustrates a jealous mockery of the friars and their comfortable way of life. John Knox commented that 'the Franciscans in Perth were very well provided for, but the like abundance was not in the Blackfriars, and yet they had more than became men professing poverty'.

The Redfriars

The only house of Trinitarians ever examined is the one just outside Dunbar (East Lothian); they are known as Redfriars because they wore a red cross on their habit. The Trinitarians were not really friars, but rather a religious order originally established to support poor pilgrims and to ransom captives in the Holy Land. A standard establishment was of three priests and three lay brethren under a prior. They were neither a mendicant nor a teaching order, but the very long church found during the excavations at Dunbar might confirm that the Trinitarians were also keen on preaching to large congregations. The house in Dunbar was established *c.* 1240; this and other Trinitarian establishments on the east coast were sited on the pilgrimage routes to St Andrews. As well as looking after pilgrims they nursed the poor, and were responsible for the Maison Dieu Hospital in Dunbar.

The church was 39m (129ft) long, with a large central tower provided with buttresses and a double-stepped chamfered base of good ashlar. The chancel was subdivided by two walls, the first of which, found near the west end, may have been the original east end of an earlier chapel extended to the east by the friars. An earlier chapel would not have required as large a chancel as that needed by the friars to accommodate their choir-stalls. The chancel floor was replaced *c.* 1500 by good-quality yellow and green tiles imported from the Netherlands.

Trial trenching around the church produced no other ranges of buildings, although an enclosing ditch was found 22m (73ft) to the south. This marked the limit of burials within the churchyard. If this was a small foundation, a standard cloister may not have been required for so few brethren. The documentary evidence shows that this chapter of Trinitarians was no longer in existence by 1529.

The Greyfriars

Unlike the other friaries discussed above, the house of the Observantine Greyfriars (reformed Franciscans) founded in 1500 at Jedburgh (**22**) was not established long enough to enjoy periods of relative peace and prosperity. The completed friary had the church on the south side with the cloister to the north. This may have been because the friars worshipped in an existing chapel until the completion of their own church to the south, after which the earlier chapel was incorporated into the north range.

The excavations here and at Linlithgow were large scale, and consequently have produced the most informative results. As at Linlithgow, a long preaching church was found, 38m (125ft) in length. The main door into the church from the cloister was found at the south-east corner of the cloister alley. Close by was the entrance to the night-stair, down from the friars' dormitory on the first floor of the east range. The base of an external garderobe block was found in the angle between the east end of the church and the east range. The rest of the layout of this range also conformed to that of Linlithgow, with a small sacristy, a chapter house to the north of that, and another smaller chamber to the north of the chapter house.

The drainage arrangement on the east side of the site included a substantial stone-lined channel fed by subsidiary drains from the cloister. Another drain was found running from the north-east corner of the cloister alley which was fed by a sump at this point, presumably draining the *lavatorium*, or washbasin, outside the doorway into the north-range refectory. The church and east range seemed to have been built at much the same time, with the north range being secondary. The kitchen may have been at the east end, divided by a partition from the main body of the north range, with a low dais for the high

22 *Jedburgh friary; reconstruction showing the friary c. 1520.*

table at the west end. A double-chambered garderobe block and chute were found at the north-east corner of the north range. This drained into the lade to the east, which was strongly revetted on either side at this point. The reredorter was probably two storey and linked directly to the dormitory. The west range consisted of one major wall against which was built a range of lean-to buildings. Beyond this was a cobbled yard between the west range and the west precinct wall.

The east boundary of the site was formed by the Skiprunning burn from which the friars took a lade to flush their main drain. Part of the burn was excavated and found to have been provided with a stone revetment on the east bank. A group of pits was found cutting the west bank, and these pits provided some fascinating botanical material, the damage caused during attacks having sealed waste assemblages within the pits. These were primarily rubbish-pits, which were found to contain apple/pear pips and other remains which may indicate production of cider. In addition, some possible medicinal plants were found including, unusually, violets which had various medicinal uses. The pits contained some faecal material, which is strange because the friary was well equipped with latrines, and so cesspits would have been unnecessary. The use of these pits as toilets may identify the aftermath of an attack, when the complex was partly in ruins.

The pits also produced valuable information concerning the friars' diet. No evidence for freshwater fish was found here or at Jedburgh Abbey, indicating that sea-fish was probably cheap and readily available. Moreover, the topography may not have been suitable for creating fish-ponds, and the fishing on the rivers Jed and Teviot would have been jealously guarded by lordly sportsmen. Sea-fish were certainly brought to the friary whole and prepared in the kitchens. The friars' life-style required them to be vegetarian; although fish would have been acceptable to their regime, the large quantities of meat, represented by the animal bones, certainly were not. Like Jedburgh Abbey, the friary was caught up in the politics of border warfare, and was attacked and badly damaged in 1523, 1544 and 1545. The friary may never have been reoccupied after the last attack.

The end of an era

The excavated and historical evidence points to the friars and their friaries as being primary targets of the Protestant reformers. The explanation of this is simple: the Reformation began in towns and the friars occupied easily accessible urban sites. Their churches were not essential for the parishioners, and they were no doubt seen as a financial burden. In addition to this, the reformers were especially wary of those friars who were closely involved with the universities, and posed a specific counter-Reformation intellectual threat. The fact that these were prime urban sites, ripe for redevelopment, also helps explain why fragments of only 6 of the original 53 friaries can now be seen.

CHAPTER THREE

Churches and cathedrals

Much of the religious and social life of the people of medieval Scotland revolved around the parish churches. It is therefore unfortunate that so few of these have been investigated compared to the disproportionate study of 'special' monastic sites. To the medieval Scot, the parish church was where you were christened, married and buried, all too often in fairly rapid succession. The church was a beacon of hope in an otherwise hard life with an uncertain future. So it is reasonable to suggest that to understand the churches brings us closer to understanding the parishioners.

It was David I (1124–53) who effectively started to create a parochial system, and revived the system of territorial dioceses, in the second quarter of the twelfth century. The bounds of a parish were often coextensive with those of an existing or newly created estate. About 1100 parish churches eventually existed, mostly concentrated in the Lowlands, only a small proportion of which now survive in anything resembling their medieval form. Many had dependent chapels, mainly built in outlying areas. A parish might also contain one or more proprietary chapels in or near the castles of the nobility.

But this is only part of the story; there were many other elements which made up the 'holy landscape' which the people inhabited, most of which have survived even less well than the churches. Within any parish might be one or more holy wells, springs and trees, associated with miracles or attributed healing powers. Free-standing carved stone crosses, including those of the earlier Christian era, would also have acted as local places of worship, preaching, veneration and even burial, for a dispersed community.

Landscape and place-name studies can help piece together the general picture of the religious features of rural parishes, but the church was always the most important part, and archaeology can help to provide the detail of how any church developed and how it looked to the parishioners. Excavations have been successful in identifying a range of outer structures which rarely survive above ground. The church was enclosed by a bank or wall, encircling the churchyard. We know that the churchyard was a centre for social activities, especially during feast days when fairs and merriment took place here. The churchyard might also contain the priest's house and maybe a latrine. A teind barn is likely to have existed near every church, being needed to store the teinds presented in the form of produce. A good example can be seen at Whitekirk (East Lothian) (**23**), and another has been excavated at Kebister (Shetland).

Due to the destruction at the time of the Reformation, the internal fittings and decoration of the medieval churches are almost completely lost to us, with excavations providing a few clues. As in monastic churches we know that the walls were rendered with lime

23 *Medieval parish church and teind barn, Whitekirk.*

mortar, with internal decoration including murals and richly painted stonework. Even the poorest parish church had glazed windows, and many would have a bellcote with a small bronze bell to summon the flock.

The priest's house is unlikely to have been a grand building as the rural clergy were generally poor, with the income appropriated to a monastery or cathedral, leaving barely enough for the upkeep of the fabric and an income for the priest. By contrast the canons of the great cathedrals were accommodated in some style in their own houses and gardens near to the church. A rare surviving example is Provands Lordship by Glasgow Cathedral.

Linlithgow chapel and vicarage

Very unusually a priest's house was uncovered at Linlithgow, close to the thirteenth-century chapel discovered beneath the later Carmelite friary. The chapel was large, measuring 21m (70ft) by 8m (27ft), and was subsequently transformed into the nave of the friary church. The priest's house was near the west door, having been built on the site of a construction-phase mason's shed. The timber house was small with a floor hearth, and would have looked no different from many timber-framed houses of the time. The good water supply and sanitary arrangements, however, do identify the house with a special user. A well was found with an overflow channel which flushed a latrine inside a small hut, with a seat raised above a stone tank. The priest's house went out of use when the friary was built, but the latrine was kept, possibly for use by the congregation.

The Hirsel

Excavations at the Hirsel (Berwickshire) have produced a unique insight into the development of an estate church in the Borders, from the tenth to the fourteenth century. This is a very interesting case as the church was identified by the discovery during ploughing of numerous fragments of medieval graveslabs and pieces of sculpted crosses. The site was then pin-pointed by geophysical survey and excavated.

The church had already been in use for some time when the original structure was considerably enlarged during the twelfth century (phase 3), by extending the nave to the west (24). At this time the church may have

24 *The Hirsel church during excavation, with apsidal east end of pre-twelfth-century church with later extensions to the west.*

belonged to a lordly family based at a nearby earth-and-timber castle. The lord's family, servants, and some of the local population may all have used the church and were buried here. The foundations were clay bonded, reserving mortar for the superstructure and for use as a floor base. The rebuilding took place just before or around the time that records show that the church and its income were presented to the newly founded house of Cistercian nuns nearby at Coldstream. Remains of a priest's house were found to the north of the Hirsel church.

Further development of the church may be associated with another historical event: in the middle of the thirteenth century, David Bernham, the Bishop of St Andrews, set about the rededication of all the churches in his diocese, including the Hirsel. A dividing wall across the chancel was removed and the west wall was rebuilt, making the church a total of 24m (80ft) in length. The thickening of the west wall was probably to support a bell-tower, the evidence for which was reinforced by the discovery of a bell-casting pit. This was the highpoint of the development of the church, probably thanks to the continued patronage of the local nobility (25).

The church was surrounded by an enclosed cemetery where over 345 graves were excavated. A favoured burial place for children was along the outside of the north wall. One burial of thirteenth- or fourteenth-century date was especially interesting: an individual had been buried with a pierced scallop shell, the badge of a pilgrim, as also seen with a burial on the Isle of May (p. 28).

The development of any church is a good barometer of the fortunes of the proprietor and of the surrounding countryside, so in this border location it is no surprise to find that the church was in decay by the fourteenth century. All or part of the church was converted into domestic accommodation, initially maybe for the priest. The final phase of use was probably when the nave was converted

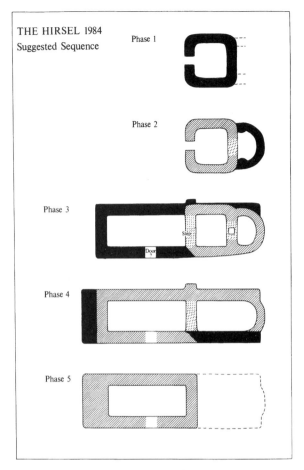

THE HIRSEL 1984
Suggested Sequence

Phase 1

Phase 2

Phase 3

Phase 4

Phase 5

25 *The Hirsel church; progression of an estate church from the tenth to the fourteenth century.*

The religious origins of the site may date back to the eighth century, and by the tenth or eleventh century there was probably a timber oratory here. The whole site was not excavated, and the remains of other structures to the west of the church may have been the residence of the Hiberno-Norse lord and his household, or else an early monastery. The site is complex and the large area around the church enclosed by a bank and ditch would seem to be too large simply to contain the church and cemetery.

A rectangular stone church was built in the middle of the twelfth century, measuring 12m (40ft) by 6m (20ft), half the length of the Hirsel. This small, well-built structure gives a helpful vision of what many similar chapels probably looked like in the Scottish countryside (**26**). This was built of stone with clay bonding, and a solid gable-wall at either end. The roof was further supported by two wooden crucks, which divided the interior into three bays. The cruck construction was identified by the discovery of the padstones which the roof timbers rested on. The mid and west bay had a clay floor, while the east chancel bay was paved in stone. Of great interest was the discovery of part of the altar, built against the east wall. Relics, in the form of bones of local saints, were found within the clay bonding of the altar. Another detail was a recess found in the north-east corner, which may have been for a sacristy chest for storing communion vessels and vestments (**27**). The east cruck could well have incorporated a screen, with a door through this giving access to the raised floor of the chancel. A wooden bench was supported on two stones which protruded from the north wall of the chancel. A padlock bolt was found in the clay floor, which would have come from a chest or a door. A more surprising find in the floor was a fragment of chainmail. Might a lord have been buried here in his armour?

At the end of the twelfth century the church was damaged by a fire and partly demolished.

into a barn, in the fifteenth or sixteenth century, which then burnt down. The evidence for this use came in the form of large amounts of carbonized grain, and pellets excreted by owls roosting in the roof trusses.

Barhobble

Barhobble (Wigtown) was a lost church which actually survived as unrecognized ruins. Parts of the jigsaw were all pieced together by careful detective work to locate the site, the clues being: stray finds of cross-slabs, a holy well nearby, roads that converged on the site, and a medieval fair which used to be held in the vicinity.

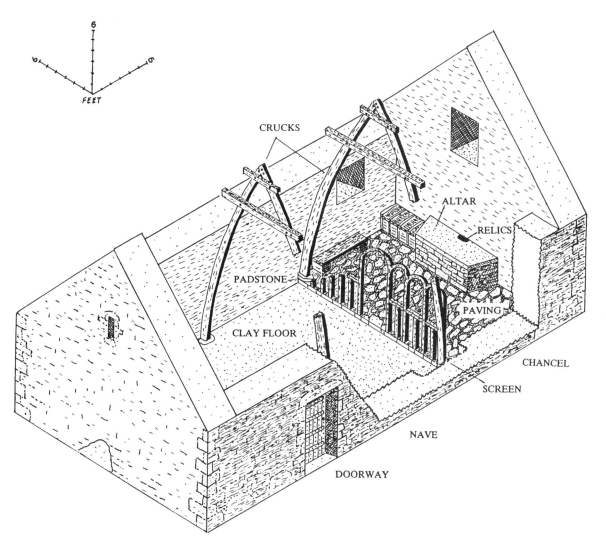

26 *Reconstruction of Barhobble church in the twelfth century.*

This was around the time that a parish church was built nearby at Mochrum, which may have taken on some of the functions of Barhobble. Soon after, Barhobble was rebuilt as a smaller chapel, formed from the two east bays, while the west bay became the chaplain's quarters. The chapel was in decay early in the fourteenth century.

Cockpen parish church

The excavations at Cockpen (Midlothian) serve as a useful illustration of how well-designed, limited excavations, linked to an above-ground structural survey can elucidate the development of a small parish church. Like so many, this is in ruins and has served a sepulchral function in more recent times. By digging in the middle of this long church, the original west wall was found (28), along with parts of a demolished Romanesque rounded arch with chevron decoration, dated to the twelfth century. The east half of the building was the original church, which measured 10m (33ft) by 5m (17ft). Examination of the standing east gable revealed that this had been

rebuilt in the thirteenth century with twin lancet windows surmounted by an oculus, or round window. This was all good-quality work, which cannot be said of the western extension which was added not long after. This is curious, as an enlargement might reasonably be connected with an increase in population and therefore church income. But it is clear that other factors were involved as the archaeological evidence pointed to a period of ruination beginning some time during the mid- to late fourteenth century. When compared to the documentary evidence, this coincides with the granting of the church to Newbattle Abbey in 1356, an action which may have been intended to revitalize the fortunes of the parish. At this time the privations of the Wars of Independence and the Black Death might both be cited to explain why a parish and its church were in decline.

St Magnus, Birsay – Christchurch of the sagas?

Christianity returned officially to Orkney as late as 955, and so the churches here arose within a very different cultural tradition. The excavations at St Magnus in the village of Birsay, in the north-west of mainland Orkney, have exposed the remains of a twelfth-century church, built on the site of a tenth-century timber oratory. Here we can see continuity of use emerging as a common feature, as also witnessed at Hirsel and Barhobble. And just as early church sites were reused by later medieval church builders, so these churches often exist hidden beneath post-medieval churches, as was the case at Birsay. This site is

27 *Barhobble church; altar (left foreground) with adjacent recess for a sacristy chest.*

28 *Cockpen church; excavations revealed the primary west wall shown here in the foreground. The east half formed the original twelfth-century church.*

not to be confused with the nearby Brough of Birsay, a tidal island which has been excavated to reveal a Pictish and Norse settlement with a twelfth-century church. (Other late Norse churches are discussed by Anna Ritchie in her book in this series entitled *Viking Scotland*.)

The excavations at St Magnus showed that the oratory had been rebuilt in stone, and subsequently extended by turning this into the chancel and building a new nave to the west in the eleventh century. At some time in the twelfth century a new church was built in the Romanesque style with good-quality architectural mouldings, showing influence from outside the insular tradition (**29**). The rebuilt church was no larger than its predecessor, being about 12m (39ft) in length. This discovery, close to the fifteenth-century bishop's palace, has opened an interesting debate concerning the identification of the church and its importance relative to the church on the Brough. The *Orkneyinga Saga* tells how Earl Thorfinn built a fine minster called Christchurch at Birsay early in the twelfth century, and that this became the first resting-place of the murdered St Magnus in 1117. The dedication of the church on the Brough to St Peter militates against this being the minster. Christchurch became part of a devotional round for pilgrims, along with other churches nearby associated with the saint. So all of these points indicate that this was a church of some importance, no doubt rebuilt by the masons invited to Orkney to build the great cathedral and shrine of St Magnus in Kirkwall. Although small, Christchurch was important; patronized by earls and bishops, and serving as the burial place, albeit temporary, of a saint.

St Ronan's – the medieval parish church of Iona

Iona is a complex liturgical landscape imbued with sanctity and meaning, much of which is lost to us now. The entire island was holy, and

29 *St Magnus church; the pre-twelfth-century chancel (middle and back) rebuilt in the twelfth century with chamfered plinth at the junction of the new nave with the north wall of the chancel.*

there were numerous especially sacred structures and natural features associated with Columba and other saints going back many centuries. The parish church, now in ruins, was located close to the focus of secular settlement by the boat-landing. This church was found to have been built on top of a small chapel with clay-bonded walls and mortar-rendered surfaces. This may have been roofed with thatch. Its appearance was much like that of other early excavated churches, such as Candida Casa (Whithorn) and Ardwall (Kirkcudbright). The excavations uncovered a possible fragment of the altar table of this early chapel, incised with equal-armed crosses.

The parish church, built *c.* 1200, incorporated the early chapel, which must have been standing in some form at the time, within its east end. This was built around the same time as the Augustinian nunnery located only 30m (100ft) to the south. Their proximity indicates a close relationship, and it is likely that a priest from the nunnery served as vicar to the parishioners.

Burgh churches

The burgh parish churches were patronized chiefly by the burgesses and by the guilds. St Nicholas, Aberdeen is a good example in that the upkeep of the nave was financed solely by the townsfolk, to the jealous exclusion of any aristocratic patrons. As the burghs developed, the churches attracted numerous endowments from burgesses and guilds, often involving the construction of chantry and guild chapels and altars within the burgh kirk. The addition of these regularly resulted in the enlargement and replanning of the churches, identifiable in excavations. There were of course numerous other chapels and churches in the burghs, including the friary churches and the chapels of almshouses, hospitals and pilgrims' hostels. Provision for parochial worship was made in most of the cathedrals and in some of the great monasteries.

The burgh churches have tended to be in continuous use, being substantially remodelled in post-medieval times, and are rarely the subject of excavations. A small excavation in the north transept and crossing of St Nicholas, Aberdeen helped to confirm the existence of a substantial Romanesque church here, dedicated to the patron saint of sailors, underlining the importance of maritime trade. Part of one of the original crossing piers was found in association with a silver halfpenny of Malcolm IV (1153–65). By 1200 the church was very large and about 70m (233ft) in length. St Nicholas was sited at the north end of the early focus of the burgh, which ran uphill to the church from the harbour. Records tell that only the church and the stone palace of William the Lion survived the great fire of 1244.

Glasgow Cathedral

Glasgow Cathedral was one of the richest in the realm; the bishops were leading politicians, and this was the administrative centre for extensive estates and numerous parishes. This ancient site contained the shrine and relics of St Mungo, or Kentigern. Much of the cathedral that stands today was begun c. 1240 and completed at the end of the thirteenth century. Excavations have set out to find evidence of the earlier cathedrals, and to discover more about the selection of the site in relation to the stage-managing of pilgrimage (**colour plate 8**).

The church is on two levels, with a crypt at the east end cleverly designed so as to allow natural light to focus on St Mungo's shrine. Excavations in the nave revealed that the earlier cathedrals also had a crypt, so that the churches on this site had always been positioned to take advantage of a steep slope. The excavations revealed the west fronts of two twelfth-century cathedrals; the earliest recorded church being that of Bishop John, whose building was consecrated, although not necessarily completed, in 1136. The chamfered base course of the west end was found, along with a number of massive half-column drums, which formed part of this earlier crypt. Part of an early twelfth-century cross-head was uncovered, which may have been a gable roof finial on this or on an even earlier church. The length of this cathedral is unknown, but was small by later standards. The excavations produced many fragments of late twelfth-century carved and decorated stonework, which are helpful when trying to picture the brightly dressed and decorated interior (**30**).

The next version of the building was begun by Bishop Joceline c. 1181. The north and south walls were of uneven lengths, suggesting that this building was never completed. Worship had to continue amid this building site, however uncomfortable, as was well illustrated by the unique discovery of what seemed to be a temporary west end made of timbers set in massive socketed stones.

Excavations in the crypt around St Mungo's tomb proved that this was newly completed in the later thirteenth century, rather than being the location of the earlier shrine. The excavations uncovered the massive pier foundations which support the piers of the choir above, taking much of the weight of the entire

31 *Cast bronze mortar of thirteenth-century date from Glasgow Cathedral, inscribed with the name of Bishop William.*

30 *Glasgow Cathedral; west front of Bishop John's cathedral consecrated in 1136, showing chamfered plinth course.*

cathedral. An extraordinary discovery was made in a trench just to the east of the shrine: two large bronze mortars and an iron pestle had been secretly buried at the time of the Reformation. They were cast vessels, each *c.* 27cm (11in) in diameter, and one was inscribed with the name of William Wishart, who was bishop from 1270 to 1272. This mortar had a convex base, and may have been held in a stand. They must have had a liturgical use, probably for mixing incense – it is known that the dean had to prepare 900g (2lb) of incense for the annual feast of St Mungo alone (31).

This fortunate survival serves to remind us of the wealth and variety of church fixtures and fittings lost at the Reformation, the knowledge of which can help enormously in understanding more of the functioning of religious life.

CHAPTER FOUR

Towns

The familiar character of many Scottish towns and cities is the legacy of our medieval forebears who planned and built the burghs. Every day, without realizing it, we walk on streets and along property boundaries created over 700 years ago; all that might be apparent now is a medieval street name. Archaeology has contributed hugely to our understanding of medieval towns, especially from the rescue excavations in Aberdeen and Perth which started in the early 1970s in response to a building boom. These two burghs are important because excavators encountered damp, well-sealed deposits which were anaerobic, that is, sealed in such a way so as to be free of oxygen and thus free of the bacteria which would normally devour organic remains. So in some of these sites a wealth of detail of artefacts and structures has survived, which make up a much fuller picture of the lives of the people translated through their personal possessions, food debris, clothes, furniture, houses and the products of their crafts. So we can describe towns and their environment with greater clarity and certainty than we can any other sites in medieval Scotland (32).

32 Reconstruction of Perth in the fourteenth century with the River Tay in the foreground.

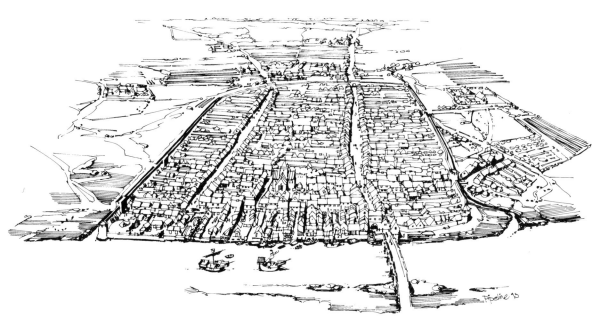

Origins and planning

Towns were formally created by David I and his successors in the twelfth century, and must be considered in the context of a contemporary, pan-European episode of urban growth. Some of the seeds of urbanism were already in place in Scotland, and so the granting of 'burgh' status would have made little immediate impact on places like Berwick, Perth, St Andrews, Dunfermline, Edinburgh, Stirling and Glasgow. Here we can simply see the formalization of stable settlements which had grown in response to economic opportunities offered by seats of government and religion. The real revolution was in the creation of a mercantile trading economy, stimulating increased agricultural production, and resulting in the abandonment of the traditional subsistence economy of the countryside. Growth in the countryside in turn stimulated growth of towns, accelerating the spread of innovation, with a greater demand for manufactured goods and services.

The rewards to the crown were manifold: they could devolve aspects of local government to a reliable merchant class, while at the same time reaping the benefits of increased taxation revenue resulting from the stimulation of agriculture, manufacturing and trade. In the second half of the twelfth century the extension of royal power was consolidated by the creation of burghs in Moray and Galloway following unsuccessful revolts. Not all burghs were founded by the crown, however; magnates and bishops also had the power to confer trading privileges.

In general terms the process of creating burghs was rapid and successful, aided by an influx of urban merchants and craftsmen from England, France, Germany and the Low Countries. The principal townsfolk were called 'burgesses', and they were granted an effective monopoly on the marketing of goods and produce from a specified large area of the surrounding countryside.

The results from numerous excavations in Perth, including the most important urban site in Scotland excavated on the north side of the High Street between 1975 and 1977, would seem to uphold the above premise. Perth experienced rapid, early development, generating considerable wealth, some of which was absorbed in obtaining luxury items through an extensive foreign trade network. Excavations on the south side of the High Street have illuminated the origins of the town; a primary ditch lined with a wattle fence was uncovered, which produced a radiocarbon date of *c.* AD 1000. So there may have been a proto-urban settlement, stretching 150m (500ft) from here to the Tay shore harbour, and associated with an early church later replaced by the burgh church of St John.

This site was then overlain in the early to mid-twelfth century by a regular pattern of property boundaries. The formal creation of a street plan, and the laying out of regularly sized plots, has been recorded at a number of early burghs and does indicate a degree of central planning by embryonic town councils or royal officers. Initially, each plot comprised a frontage house with a long, narrow piece of land behind, known as a backland or rig. The burgh boundaries were also demarked, in some cases with defensive banks, ditches, or walls. Morphology and scale were often influenced by natural constraints, such as hills and streams.

The street pattern of some early towns grew out from a single main street linking two key institutions such as the burgh church and a royal castle. In other cases, such as St Andrews, a parallel grid system was laid down. The market place was centrally located at the heart of the burgh, sometimes at the intersection of two main streets.

Streets and houses

The main streets were roughly metalled with gravel and small stones, but with much of the

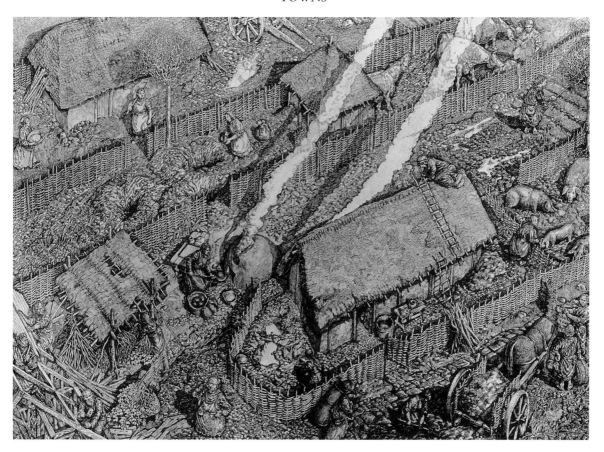

33 Reconstruction of backlands in Aberdeen c. *1300.*

surface comprising rubbish which had been dumped there. Uniformity of excavated street surfaces suggests that the main streets at least were maintained by the burgh council. These were not all narrow, and excavations in Perth have shown that the High Street was 4m (14ft) wider in the twelfth and thirteenth centuries than it is today. It was soon encroached on in later centuries when there was a greater pressure on land. Along the market streets of some towns, the houses were set back behind a paved foreland where temporary or permanent stalls would have stood. The frontage was not the only position for the best houses, and the few frontages which have been investigated have revealed some modest structures. Frontages rarely survive, however, due to the continual redevelopment of these prime sites,

and the construction of deep cellars in more recent times.

Just as the frontages contained a mixture of some of the best and some of the poorer houses, the same is also true of the backlands. Access was by a pend through or between the houses on the frontage to a common close which ran between the backlands. Where pressure on land was strong, houses of varying quality and status of occupants would run together along a rig to create a terrace with party walls. An important image to capture is that of how dynamic and fluid the appearance of town centres was; building techniques and materials dictated that houses had to be rebuilt every few years, and often did not last longer than twenty years. Excavations have shown that destruction by fire was very common. The location of property plots or rigs was also fluid, and in some cases these were being redefined two or three times every hundred years, chiefly as a result of change in ownership (33).

The vast majority of houses were small, single-storey wooden structures, or at least this is true of the two hundred or so houses which have been excavated. Of these a quarter of the total sample are from one site on the north side of the High Street in Perth. Here and elsewhere the townsfolk made good use of the locally available organic materials to build simple but adequate homes, byres and workshops. Most of the excavated houses were 7–8m (22–26ft) in length by 3–4m (10–13ft) in width, running axially along the narrow backland plots. The majority were created by building a framework of upright stakes around which were woven thin, flexible branches or 'withies', to create wattle walls. The same trees were exploited for structural timbers, and in addition to these the much prized oak provided about half of the total. The quality of the wattle-work varied considerably, although the walls were rarely seen as they were usually clad with clay, dung, mud, peat or turf. If an end wall was left unclad then this may have been to provide better ventilation for a byre. Sometimes a double-skin wall was made for extra insulation (34).

A standard construction method from the thirteenth century onwards was the use of a sill beam which was lain horizontally on a rough stone foundation. This technique stopped the wood from rotting so quickly, which was a serious problem when uprights were held fast in the damp earth. Sills have been found with grooves to hold plank walls or with sockets to support a wattle frame-work. Good, long timbers were needed to make sills, and these were clearly at a pre-mium, so savings could be made by building the non-structural gable-walls using only stake and wattle. Lengths of timber, usually no more than 3m (10ft) long, were jointed together with simple lap joints to create the foundations of long walls. A group of well-

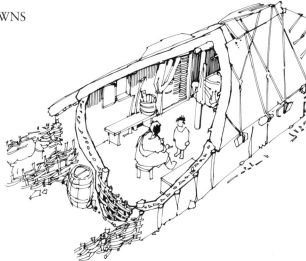

34 *Reconstruction of a typical wattle house from twelfth-century Perth.*

built burgesses' houses of the fourteenth and fifteenth centuries were excavated in Castle Street, Inverness, and these seem to have had sills on the frontage walls only. Some preserved sections of vertical oak-plank walling were found here.

Walls would have stood no more than 1.5m (5ft) high, capped by a roof plate of roughly shaped branches, joined together, which supported the principal rafters of the roof. Sometimes the roof plate, or more simply the rafters only, were supported on external load-bearing posts. Forked oak posts at the gable ends would have supported a ridge pole, again probably formed from lengths of timber lashed or jointed together. The more substantial timber houses were strong enough to support a roof covered with glazed ceramic peg-tiles or thin stone roof-slabs, but the majority of houses were roofed with thatch of rushes, broom, heather or straw. Ropes weighted down with flat stones could have helped hold the thatch in place. Wooden shingles were another alternative, and would have provided a more durable organic covering. In many cases, only the ridge and the area around the smoke-hole may have been tiled to give extra protection from the weather. Gable ends of tiled roofs were sometimes decorated with ceramic finials (35).

Doorways were usually placed off-centre in one of the long walls and provided with a planked or cobbled threshold. Doors would have been made of planks, and could be locked; security was a concern and simple padlocks are a common find, being used on doors and to secure internal cupboards and chests (**36**). Windows would have been small and equipped with wooden shutters.

Inside were floors of sand, clay or gravel, covered with bracken, straw or heather (**37**). Timber floors have also been found. Botanical examination of earth floors has shown that these could be sweetened by the addition of meadowsweet, an aromatic herb. As floors built up one on top of the other, and houses were regularly rebuilt, the lower surfaces and debris would have provided a progressively drier foundation for each successive house. Perth was naturally boggy and experienced flash floods, so there may have been a conscious effort to raise the town up on its

36 *A medieval barrel padlock from Perth.*

own rubbish, 3m (10ft) in less than 250 years in some places (**colour plate 9**). The other side of this coin was subsidence, as witnessed on the High Street site in Perth, where a dynamic building pattern, coupled with changes to property boundaries and pressure on what had been open backlands, meant that new houses were built over infilled, but uncompacted rubbish-pits! Animals shared the same roof as people, and the byre end can be identified when a stony floor with a drain is found. Some houses had an internal hearth within a shallow clay-lined pit or else flush with the floor on a flat stone, even though such hearths were a fire hazard in thatched wooden houses (**38**). External cooking hearths are also found.

People would have had furniture according to their wealth; benches and trestles being most common. The remarkable assemblage of preserved wood found on the High Street, Perth included turned stool legs (**39**). Some of the large numbers of feathers found on the

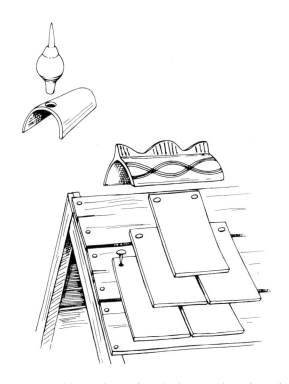

35 *Durable roofing: glazed tiles, a ridge tile and a finial.*

37 *Sand floor within a twelfth-century wattle house in the High Street, Perth, with a byre attached to the south gable, and the wattle wall of another building to the west (right).*

38 (Below) *Reconstructed interior of a wattle house c. 1300.*

same site might have come from burgesses' feather-bedding. Lighting was afforded by candles made of sheep's fat, and ceramic lamps fuelled with linseed oil.

Neighbours – a slice across three rigs at Kirk Close, Perth

This excavation allows us to see who was living next door to each other across three parallel rigs in a mid-backland area, 17m (54ft) distant from the High Street frontage, during the thirteenth and fourteenth centuries (**40**). The westernmost of the three was a post-and-wattle house, at least 5m (16ft) long by at least 3m (10ft) wide, built along the rig. This had a clean sand floor except for a narrow strip at the south (back) end, where an earth floor identified an animal stall. A large burnt stone formed the base of a hearth. A doorway gave access on to a wide gravel path which separated this house from the middle of the three excavated; the path marked the property boundary.

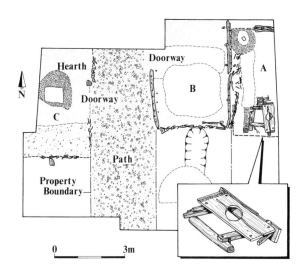

40 Three houses and the latrine in the thirteenth century at Kirk Close, Perth.

The middle house also ran along the rig and was sited slightly further north than the first. This was 7m (23ft) long, constructed with sill beams laid directly on the ground for the long east and west walls. The east sill was formed from two beams with a simple lap joint. The roof was supported by posts inside the long walls. An insubstantial wattle wall separated this from the next plot to the east, with only a small gap between the two houses. Their south end walls were on the same line, but the eastern house ran across the width of the rig, which must have been in excess of 6m (20ft). This house had big squared corner posts of oak, again with sill beams resting on earth as foundations for the stake-and-wattle long walls. The gable walls were also stake-and-wattle, but woven around earthfast posts. The most important feature of this house was an internal latrine tucked into the south-west corner. Here a timber-framed pit was found, made from reused oak timbers, and incredibly the oak plank toilet seat survived *in situ*. It was secured by a peg at each corner, and had a band of crudely incised decoration at the north end facing into the room. The pit was full of moss (toilet tissue). The user would have sat looking east, and may have preserved their

39 Twelfth/thirteenth-century stool legs.

modesty by being hidden behind a wattle partition which was found collapsed on the north side. Botanical analysis identified the areas to the north and south of the houses as being used as stockyards and domestic middens.

Initially, this eastern house was of the most expensive construction with oak load-bearing posts and a posh internal loo. The house in the middle plot was built of softwoods, but in turn was superior to the western house of even poorer construction, shared with animals. This situation was reversed, however, later on in the fourteenth century when the middle and eastern houses were demolished, and a large rubbish-pit was dug on the site of the middle house, with a wattle cover which rested on four large poles (41). At about this time the western house became a cobbler's workshop, before being replaced by an increasingly large and sophisticated house with sill beams resting on stone foundations. This was enlarged with a dwelling at the front and a stone-paved

41 Excavating the collapsed wattle rubbish-pit cover at Kirk Close, Perth.

bakery at the rear, with the gravel path providing access for carts from the High Street. Silks were found in the baker's house, along with a macehead indicating that he was a burgess with duties of guarding the town (42). The empty plots to the east may hint at there being less pressure on land compared to 100 years before.

A long hall from the High Street, Perth

Among the many houses found in these backland plots were at least three grand timber-framed buildings. These are called long halls, and usually had internal roof supports sometimes creating an aisled plan. The most complete example was built here *c.* 1250, located centrally within a line of buildings running axially along the rig away from the frontage. This hall was originally 12m (38ft) long by 5.5m (18ft) wide, with two rows of internal roof supports. The external walls were of wattle and daub (baked clay and dung), and the interior was divided into two rooms by a wattle partition. The exalted

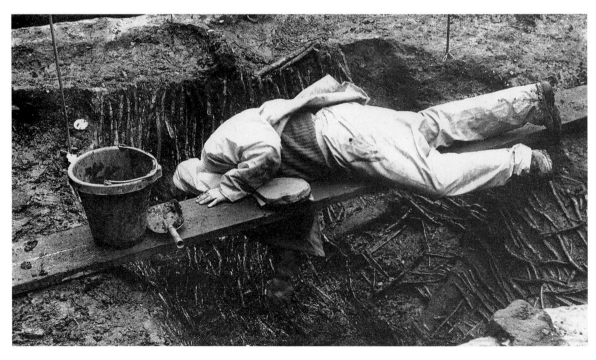

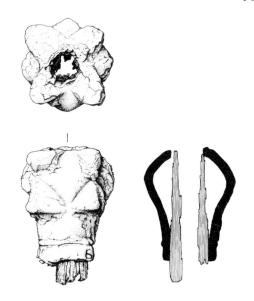

42 *Baker's macehead, from Kirk Close, Perth.*

status of the burgess owner (or was this the town house of a knight?) was confirmed by finds of pottery imported from Rouen in France, along with a spur. The latter would suggest that this building might have a stable at the rear. This was similar to aisled halls found in earthwork castles of the same date, for example at Rattray (p. 93).

This hall burnt down and was replaced on the same site by a slightly larger house, rebuilt in such a fashion as to suggest that the owner intended to give an impression of wealth. The wall fronting on to the path which ran along the rig was rebuilt with vertical planks, just like the smaller houses in Inverness described above. Internally the hall had three rooms, with a large central chamber flanked by a single smaller chamber at each end. The back room had a hearth and may have been the kitchen; such a grand house is reconstructed here (**43**) with an external latrine chamber.

Stone houses

On the High Street site in Perth, the foundations of an early stone house were found 15m (50ft) away from the street frontage, dated to the later thirteenth century. This was a rectangular house which ran along the rig, and was 5m (18ft) in width. At this time there are likely to have been other stone houses on parts of the High Street frontage.

The surviving parts of stone walls are much more substantial than the low stone foundations constructed for wooden sill beams, and therefore the two cannot be confused. What is uncertain, however, is how tall the houses were and whether they were built of stone to full height. Many stone houses are likely to have had projecting upper floors built of timber, for instance the Kinnoul Lodging in Perth, demolished in 1966. Many were held in multiple occupancy, with each room being a separate rented property accessed from external timber galleries and stairs (**44**).

Another good example of a stone-based house was found in Edinburgh half-way between the High Street and the Cowgate, apparently built against part of the town defences in the late fourteenth century. This house ran along the rig, fronting on to Cants Close, and was well built with a tiled floor, alternating yellow, green and black in hue. The house had an integral garderobe chute from first-floor level which debouched down the steep slope to the Cowgate, where midden deposits of medieval date have been recorded

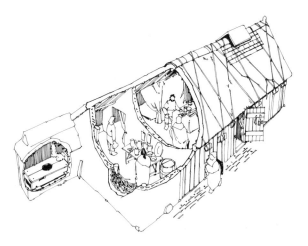

43 *Reconstruction of a thirteenth-century long hall from Perth.*

down to an incredible depth of 10m (33ft). This house was demolished in the late fifteenth century, and another house was then built immediately to the south on the same alignment.

One of the most complete plans of a stone house, dating from *c.* 1500, was found on the St Paul's Street site in Aberdeen. This free-standing building was 10m (33ft) by 7m (24ft) and built at right angles to the street frontage, which then was over 15m (50ft) away to the south. A wealthy burgess had this house built within a double-width plot, formed from what had been two separate rigs in the fourteenth century. The substantial stone foundations supported an entirely stone superstructure, probably of two floors with an attic. On the ground floor there was a partitioned passage-way which ran the length of the east side, probably affording access from front to back. At the front this would have been entered under an external stone forestair; the stair would have given access to a door in the south-east corner at first-floor level.

45 *Abbot House, Dunfermline; the fifteenth-century abbot's lodging with sixteenth-century addition (foreground), visible in the west gable.*

By the fifteenth and sixteenth centuries there were many stone houses in towns, although these were still heavily outnumbered by timber houses. The stone houses also increased in size and sophistication, with the lodgings of crown officers, lairds and clerics resembling small tower houses. An encouraging factor is that more medieval stone buildings survive than previously thought, subsumed within apparently post-medieval houses. This has been especially true in Fife, where investigations at the Abbot House in Dunfermline (p. 21), at the east end of the High Street in Kirkcaldy, and at various locations in St Andrews, have revealed substantial, hidden remains of medieval town houses (45).

The backlands

The regularity and size of properties varied considerably within and between burghs across the centuries. On some sites the property divisions are constant for centuries, while others in the same burgh were realigned every 20–50 years, and were often between 5m (16ft) and 7m (23ft) in width. The rig boundaries are found either as shallow ditches, which also had a drainage function, or as wattle fences, which doubled as stock barriers.

44 *Kinnoul Lodging, Perth; a late medieval stone house with jettied upper timber floors.*

46 *Mid-twelfth-century wattle hurdle path, running between the backland properties and the High Street, Perth.*

47 *A timber-lined drain or culvert of fourteenth-century date from Aberdeen.*

Paths are often found running along the rigs, cobbled or at least roughly metalled, and even formed from wattle hurdles in damp areas (**46**). The domestic water supply was to be found here, consisting of numerous wells and cisterns dug into the ground, and sometimes lined with reused barrels. The rig dwellers had an unfortunate habit of digging their cesspits close to the water supply, resulting in contamination. Purpose-built drains are also found, and these are difficult to distinguish from clean-water culverts. A timber-lined and covered example was found cutting across two or more plots on the St Paul's Street site in Aberdeen (**47**). This was dated to the fourteenth century, when the rigs were fairly empty

of houses. One of the most remarkable finds from the excavations at High Street, Perth was a wooden sluice gate, 440mm (18in) in width, from a culvert or drain, dated to c. 1200 (48).

The backlands had many uses: for housing, workshops, stores, keeping animals, growing food, gardens, and as rubbish-dumps. Large amounts of domestic and industrial rubbish are encountered in every backland excavation, usually found in small middens and rubbish-pits, and sometimes in very large, communal heaps. Rubbish-pits are of great value to the archaeologist as the contents may have been deposited over a relatively short period of time and then sealed, giving an insight into the lives of the people who generated the rubbish. Much of the rubbish was carted off to the town fields, although this may only have been true of the later medieval centuries when a connection was made between decaying rubbish and disease.

Very different patterns emerge when the rigs of Aberdeen and Perth are compared. In Aberdeen the rigs were generally not so

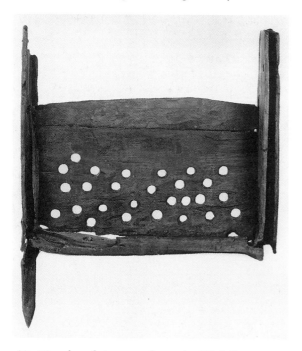

48 *Wooden sluice gate from the High Street, Perth.*

intensively developed, whereas in Perth they were heavily built up and subdivided, with many good-quality buildings owned or rented by individual proprietors. At the St Paul's Street site in Aberdeen, the opposite was suggested, in that the occupants of the wattle houses were interpreted as being poor craftsmen and their families who were dependent on the frontage owners. In Aberdeen there was less evidence of population pressure, where the backlands have been found to have been fairly empty, often just being garden ground. Here it was possible to allocate large blocks of land to the friaries, whereas in Perth it was necessary for the friars to build outside the burgh bounds. A different pattern has emerged for St Andrews in the sixteenth century, when plots were amalgamated and thick layers of garden soil were laid down. This increase in horticultural and agricultural activity seems to date from the Reformation, when the economy of St Andrews would have been knocked sideways by the removal of the established church hierarchy.

Castles and defences

More than half the rigs of a burgh terminated at the town boundaries, where defensive barriers were to be found. These ranged in severity from a line of stakes with a shallow drainage ditch, to the extremes of massive stone walls interrupted at intervals with towers. Stone walls were of course very expensive, and consequently only a handful of burghs were so equipped. Most did have stone gateways, known as ports, especially at the main entrances into the burghs, as these were customs points where dues were paid on goods brought in to market.

Burghs were located at strategic places, and 31 of the 33 towns founded by the kings of Scots before 1286 were in the shadow of royal castles. Burgesses were obliged not only to help defend the burgh, but also to maintain any defensive structures which stood at the

1 *St Adrian's Priory, Isle of May; the excavated church looking from the west entrance to the east end.*

2 *Excavating the east range at Jedburgh Abbey.*

3 *Paisley Abbey drain.*

4 *Aberdeen Carmelite Friary; excavations of the west end of the church and the cemetery.*

5 Thirteenth/fourteenth-century coloured window-glass from the church at the Aberdeen Carmelite Friary, with painted designs of leaves and fruit.

6 Thirteenth/fourteenth-century seal matrix of the Friary, found close to the Perth Carmelite church. It shows a friar kneeling under the Virgin and Child.

7 *Fragments of pottery vessels and shells from Linlithgow Carmelite Friary, used for mixing paint; and lumps of red ochre and indigo pigment, used in wall painting, panel painting and manuscript illumination.*

8 *Glasgow Cathedral; excavating the twelfth-century west fronts.*

9 *Stratigraphy in Perth: successive wooden buildings and floors – a town raised on its own muck.*

10 *A mould for casting finger-rings of fourteenth-century date from Perth.*

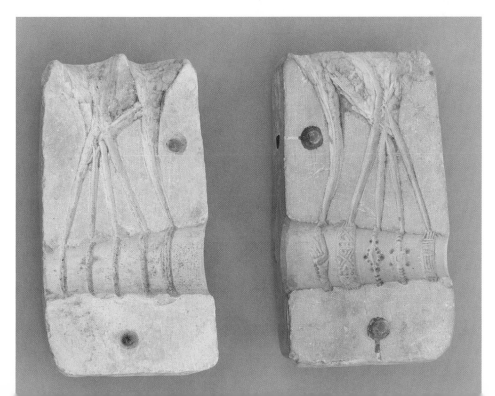

11 *Tableware from Aberdeen c.1300: pottery vessels and a wooden bowl.*

12 *A typical medieval boot, found in Perth.*

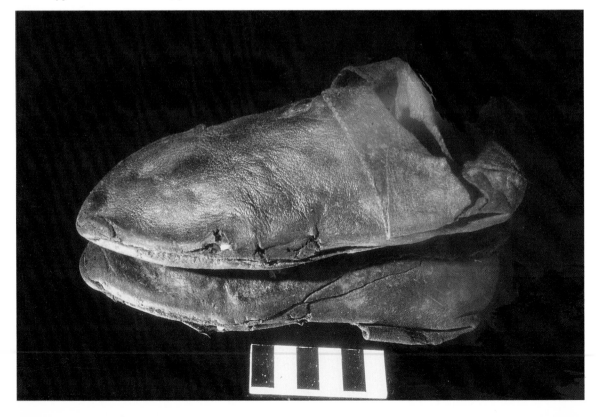

13 *Rattray motte, fourteenth-century stone hall.*

14 *Spittal of Glenshee: a head dyke running along the hillside with visible remains of house platforms and cultivations.*

15 *Buzzart Dykes deer park earthworks.*

16 *The Great Island and the Council Island, Finlaggan.*

back of their property. Towns did not have standing garrisons, so the burgesses were relied upon to perform 'watch and ward' for the king, guarding against riot and attack.

As ever, most of the evidence we have is from Perth which because of its great importance was the exception rather than the rule. It had great strategic value as the 'onlie saif and certane passage betwixt the north and south parties of this realm in all kinds of weather'. The primary twelfth-century ditch and bank has been found at two places on the northern defensive circuit, at the end of the High Street rigs, and at Mill Street to the west. The ditch may have been as much as 10m (33ft) wide with an inner bank. This was connected to the Tay, and to the earth-and-timber royal castle which was destroyed by a flood in 1209 and never rebuilt, placing greater emphasis on the town's own defences. At Mill Street, an inner stone revetment was added to the ditch in the early thirteenth century, along with a flight of rough steps (**49**).

A 23m (76ft) length of the town wall was found at the end of the High Street site. The wall survived as three courses of good ashlar. Perth changed hands a number of times during the Wars of Independence, and was held for long periods by the English. This wall may have been part of the first stone defences built in 1303–4 to the orders of Edward, Prince of Wales and slighted in 1313 by Robert Bruce.

In the later fourteenth century, 21 large stone shot were tipped into the Mill Street ditch. These were the ammunition for trebuchets, great throwing engines which might have stood on towers and gates, and which were redundant by this time. The expansion of Perth in the fourteenth century meant that

49 *Stone revetment of the Perth town ditch.*

a new western defensive circuit was required, and part of this was found at South Methven Street. Here the ditch was a massive 20m (66ft) wide by *c.* 5m (16ft) deep. The ditch was probably part of the defences ordered by Edward III, and paid for by the Prior of St Andrews along with the abbots of Lindores, Balmerino, Arbroath and Coupar Angus.

Excavations on the High Street in Edinburgh have provided good evidence for the implementation of a royal decree intended to improve the integrity of the town defences. The fourteenth-century King's Wall ran east to west, about half-way between the High Street and the Cowgate burn. The stone wall seems to have replaced an earlier line of wooden stakes. A stone house was built up against the inside of the wall in Cants Close, some time before 1400 (p. 61). The wall was subsequently altered with the addition of a stone bastion. The stone house was demolished late in the fifteenth century, *c.* 1472, when James III decreed that the 'houses biggit upon our walls be casten doun for the strengthening of the said town and the defences thereof'.

Town and country

Towns were peopled by large numbers of first-generation countryfolk, mainly servants, craftsmen and their families. Divisions between town and country were not sharply drawn, especially where unenclosed burghs merged with the surrounding fields. Each burgh had direct control of the 'croft lands' – the immediate countryside which could stretch for miles outwith the burgh. This hinterland contained the arable and pasture which was divided up among the burgesses, along with important natural resources.

But we do not have to look outside the burghs to find fields, as some existed inside the towns. In St Andrews, at the Queen Mary's House site near the cathedral, excavators found that the site had been built on during the twelfth and thirteenth centuries, but by the

fourteenth century had been abandoned and put under the plough. This might indicate that, by this time, pressure on land here had reduced, resulting in the adaption of town rigs for agricultural and horticultural use. Excavations at New Row in Dunfermline found that in the fifteenth century ploughed fields ran right up to the outside of the abbey precinct wall, before being overlain by property boundaries during the expansion of the burgh. But with most burghs, fields and orchards were located outwith the bounds, in an agricultural landscape punctuated by the farms and cottages of farmers and labourers who worked for the burgesses. Cows, sheep, goats and pigs, which were kept in town, would have been herded daily on the croft lands.

The hinterland was exploited for raw materials by craftsmen, and by the wider population for timber, other building materials, fuel and wild food. Wooden bowls are a common find on burgh excavations, and would have been produced by wood-turners working in the surrounding woodland (**50, 51**). Some industries were driven out of town due to shortage of space or because they were antisocial, such as skinning and tanning. Brothels could also come under the category of being antisocial, and so were located out of town; bawdy houses were apparently a

50 *Wooden bowls and a stave-built bucket*

51 *Excavation of the wooden bucket from Kirk Close, Perth.*

Nicholas. This isolation hospital was founded in the second half of the twelfth century, and was placed under secular, as opposed to monastic, control. Leprosy had been introduced by crusaders and pilgrims returning from the Holy Land, and by the fifteenth century there was a hospital in each of the major east-coast burghs. Excavations at the St Andrews site revealed a large enclosure which originally contained a number of timber buildings in the twelfth and thirteenth centuries. In the four-teenth century a precinct wall was built, en-closing an area at least 100m (333ft) north–south by 70m (230ft) wide. Two large stone buildings were excavated within the north part of the precinct, one being the kitchen or bakehouse (**52**). Just to the east of this was a building which could have been the infirmary hall, and this measured 26m (84ft) east–west by 15m (50ft). The location of the cemetery has been indicated by the discovery of skeletons 30m (100ft) to the north. Leper hospitals had to be self-sufficient, using produce grown in their precinct and on their own farms nearby.

Most suburban development was the overspill of housing outwith the legally defined bounds of the burgh. Burghs were constrained by their boundaries, and when populations were rising they had a number of options: they could build taller houses, they could further colonize the backlands, or else they could spill out into suburbs. The construction of suburban friaries is likely to have encouraged this process. So if we were to stand at the gates of a burgh and look out we would see four inter-dependent zones, centred on the town, with suburban housing, industry, rubbish-dumps, religious institutions, hospitals and mills all lying immediately within the shadow of the burgh bounds. Roads and paths would lead our eyes not much further out to a wider zone of town fields, scrub woodland and pasture, which looked into the town with its back to the greater countryside beyond.

considerable fire risk! Other activities were located here due to the danger of fire, including the pottery and tile industries, along with iron smithing and smelting. Water-dependent industries may have been placed outwith the burgh, either because the water supply within was restricted, or for fear of polluting the drinking supply. This would have affected tanning, brewing, cloth dyeing and fulling. The town mills, operated as a mono-poly by the burgesses, also had to be sited on water courses.

Churches, chapels, hospitals and cemeteries were located on roads leading into burghs. At major pilgrimage centres such as St Andrews and Dunfermline, inns and pilgrims' hostels would also be found. Excavations on the southern outskirts of St Andrews have iden-tified the remains of a number of these structures, including the leper hospital of St

52 *Bakehouse oven from St Nicholas leper hospital, St Andrews.*

Man and the environment

The rise of urban archaeology in the last twenty years has gone hand in hand with the retrieval of environmental data: ecofacts, as opposed to artefacts. This data provides evidence of how the townsfolk interacted with their environment, particularly in terms of how they exploited the countryside of the immediate hinterland to provide food and shelter. The data comes from samples systematically collected during excavation, sampled with explicit questions in mind. The ecofacts range from large fragments of preserved organic matter, through to microscopic pollen which can only be retrieved and identified in the laboratory. Preservation is aided by waterlogged soil conditions, or else by the material having been charred.

The environmental zones which they had direct access to were: wetland, heathland, woodland, arable and seashore. The evidence indicates that the natural products of these zones were collected by the individuals who

were to consume them, on a seasonal basis, or as and when required.

The trick to correctly interpreting the ecofacts is in identifying which were actually imported as things that were useful to man, and in filtering out the many species which appear in the samples by accident. This is singularly the case with the mass of weeds which appear in many samples, representing arable land outside the burgh, and wasteland within. Analysis of cesspits has been illuminating, showing that the people consumed large quantities of cereals, and that intestinal worms were a daily fact of life. Mosses from heath and bog were popular as toilet tissue. Moss, heather and hemp were all woven to make rope (53), and heather and bracken were collected in large quantities from heathlands in summer for use as bedding, flooring and roofing. Cereal straw and rushes were also used.

To build even a small wattle house meant the gathering of large quantities of wattles, posts and clay, along with bedding, flooring and roofing materials. The evidence suggests that the flexible withies, and more substantial poles and posts, were all coming from scrub and marginal woodland, rather than being the output of well-managed forests which were under the control of the nobility. Analysis has shown that 50 per cent of withies were hazel, the rest being alder, birch, willow, elm and apple, while 50 per cent of structural timbers were oak, along with other species including Scots pine. These required much more shaping and preparation than the withies, and the oak was so precious that it was always used more than once. So we can say that the environment determined the shape and size of the urban houses, as the builders only had access to areas of scrub, riverbank, wayside and hedges.

The bulk of the diet was cereal-based, and much of the evidence we have for this comes from the environmental evidence. The same is true of the identification of flax, grown to produce linen and linseed oil, and also the identification of plants used in dyeing cloth. These preserved plant remains help reconstruct a much fuller picture of life, including evidence of the use of medicinal plants. The potentially poisonous opium poppy, henbane and deadly nightshade were probably used to induce sleep and to relieve pain. Various plants were

prepared to treat worm infestations, including some of the mosses retrieved from the latrine in Kirk Close.

Trade

Historical evidence shows that Scotland's wealth was based on the export of raw wool, woolfells (sheepskins), hides and fish. Trade was centred on the principal east-coast burgh ports of Aberdeen, Dundee, Perth, Leith and Berwick. The documentary evidence indicates that a lot of the traffic was destined for Bruges in Flanders. Trade produced much of the wealth of the burgesses who acted as merchants, middlemen and shippers; they were therefore effectively controlling the production of these commodities in the countryside. In return, the burgesses imported a variety of manufactured goods and raw materials. Business in the burghs was regulated by the guild, which was composed of the wealthiest burgesses. A merchant's beam-balance, used for weighing coins and bullion, was found at the High Street excavations in Perth.

Archaeology can examine the evidence for the breeding and processing of the animals which formed the basis of the export trade. In addition to this, archaeology can identify the sources of the manufactured goods and luxury items which were being imported, thus building up a picture of the trade networks and routes.

The evidence for the processing of the animal products is abundant due to the large quantities of bones which are found during excavations. Interpretation is based on the relative proportions of species, and the age at which animals were slaughtered. It is important to be aware that every single part of the animal was utilized wherever possible, which means that any animal-bone assemblage is a mixture of commercial, domestic and industrial waste.

When the archaeological and historical evidence are compared there is an immediate

53 *Three-strand plaited moss rope, possibly used to tie down thatch on the roofs of the houses at Kirk Close, Perth.*

contradiction. The documents point to wool as the most important export, being in great demand by the weavers of Flanders, Picardy and Artois; whereas the excavated data clearly indicates that cattle were the most numerous animals. Nevertheless, the wool trade was important, especially for the monasteries which exported great quantities of the wool from their own flocks, and imported fine cloth in return, as shown by the discovery of foreign cloth seals at Paisley Abbey (see p. 29). All of these animals came to market on the hoof to be slaughtered in the burghs. The picture which emerges is fairly uniform from excavations in towns throughout Scotland. We see that most cattle were killed when they were about five years old, being the optimum for the production of hides. Two kill-off patterns have emerged for the less numerous sheep: some were killed aged one year or less for meat and woolfells, while others were kept on the farms until they were at least four years old having produced annual crops of wool.

Excavations have produced evidence of the items from the other side of the balance of trade, including silks from Spain and Italy, fine dyed cloth from the Low Countries, ivory and spices from Africa and even further east, and figs and grapes from the Mediterranean. Trade was also about the essentials of life, and it is recorded that grain was imported via Kings Lynn in the twelfth and thirteenth centuries, at a time when rural production had not yet caught up with the burgeoning population. While trade was direct with the countries across the North Sea and the Baltic, the evidence indicates that Scotland was also at the end of other, more complex trade networks, and so many of the exotic items had to be bought from middlemen at ports in England or abroad. Pottery is a useful indicator of trading contacts, and is another of the most common finds from urban sites. Ceramics were traded for their own qualities, or because of what they contained. The individual form and decoration of ceramics makes them easily

54 *North Sea trading links.*

identifiable as being foreign, and numerous fragments of pots from Yorkshire, Nottingham, Humberside, East Anglia, the Low Countries, France and Germany have been recorded. Some can be associated with the trade in particular commodities, for example thirteenth-century pottery from Saintonge in south-west France is likely to be related to the trade in wine from Bordeaux (54).

The fact that Scotland was chiefly an exporter of raw materials can be interpreted as meaning that the economy was poor and unstable compared to her neighbours, but the archaeological evidence would argue against this simplistic view. Excavations have shown that the burghs contained a large number of healthy industries, providing finished goods for local consumption, and no doubt for export when circumstances allowed. Scotland, like much of Europe, experienced an economic boom in the twelfth and thirteenth centuries, but found trade after this much more difficult, not least because of an effective blockade mounted by the English. As Scotland was at the end of trade networks, her merchants could not diversify into other trade zones if the eastern seaways were blocked.

Harbours

Water transport by sea and river was the best way of moving goods and people. Timbers from fairly sizeable boats have been found reused in medieval houses, and there have been two finds of paddles from smaller skin-boats and coracles, which were used for inshore fishing and as river ferries (55). Small craft would be pulled up on to a shore, but larger sailing ships required a quay or jetty. Medieval waterfronts were sometimes preserved when new quays were built, with the space between filled with silt and rubbish.

The reclamation aspect is most noticeable at Kirkwall, Orkney, where the present harbour is now some 350m (1160ft) to the north of the earlier waterfront. A number of small excavations successfully located medieval stone quays which originally stood along the west side of the main street, opposite St Magnus Cathedral and the old castle.

At Shore Brae in Aberdeen, documentary evidence from the mid-fourteenth century indicates that a timber quay stood at the highest navigable point on the Dee estuary. Excavations here uncovered a stone quay which might have replaced part of the timber one in the later fourteenth century. The quay was of tightly jointed, granite ashlar blocks with a lower face of rubble construction, all of which was bonded with clay. This impressive

waterfront survived to a depth of more than 3m (10ft), having been infilled and abandoned in the fifteenth century when a new quay was built.

The twelfth-century waterfront on the Tay at the east end of the High Street in Perth carried on in use until the nineteenth century. By the sixteenth century, however, the burgh needed a 'New Haven', part of which has been found in excavations. Construction began in 1539 at the south-east corner of the town, where a lade carried water from the Kings Mills to the Tay. Excavations showed that the mouth of the lade had been widened to form a basin, with an ashlar-faced quay built on the south side.

55 A paddle (right), similar to one excavated in Aberdeen (below), being used with a wicker coracle covered in hides.

CHAPTER FIVE

Everyday life in towns

Craft and industry

It has been estimated that as much as 30 per cent of the work-force were occupied in simply supporting the population, by providing food, clothing and shelter. Most people just scraped a living and, no matter how fascinating we find luxury foreign imports to be, we must realize that these did not play any part in the lives of the majority of townsfolk. It is clear that the development of industries was a spur for urbanization, but above all the burghs can be described in terms of being processing plants for the products of the countryside. Stirling, Inverness and Perth served as giant abattoirs, supporting a network of industries for the processing of hides, meat and bone. The presence of such a large volume of beasts in towns is attested by the great quantity of dung found in so many of the environmental samples. This emerging pattern also helps provide another counter to the simple/unstable model applied to the economy (see p. 70), in that the production of hides is in fact a key indicator of stability and long-term investment. This was because of the long timespan of 12–18 months from slaughter to the final production of leather.

Before the development of towns the crown concentrated the production and stockpiling of food in royal estates. Such stocks were essential for the court, for feeding armies, or for when famine hit. So it can be suggested that, as inspired by the crown, urbanization was the logical next step, where the royal mills and granaries were to be found, along with cooperages producing barrels essential to the airtight preservation of salted meat and fish.

Towns offered opportunities for specialist trades, like artists and goldsmiths, who might work for merchants, senior clergy, or royal officers and nobility. Most of the ordinary townsfolk, however, made their livelihood from labour-intensive production activities. Archaeology has not been able to identify many specific workshops, but has been very successful in retrieving and interpreting the remains of numerous craft and industrial activities, identified by the debris of manufacturing. Towns offered craftsmen an economy of scale: interdependent crafts could feed off each other, and work on a much larger and more profitable scale. Craftsmen practising the same trade often congregated together in one part of the burgh, as these were close-knit groups who could help each other out. Sometimes this grouping together was enforced, as in the case of fire industries. Innovation was also an important factor, allowing new ideas and technologies to spread much faster.

Animal-based industries

We have already seen that the economy was based on animals, and especially on cattle. Every part of the carcass was utilized, and cattle provided the raw materials for fleshers, tanners, leatherworkers, horners, candle-makers and a host of others. Cattle provided meat, blood, hide, guts, lard, bones and horns. Burgesses enjoyed a double monopoly, not only in controlling the export of hides and wool, but also in the marketing of the meat.

The bones exhibit ample evidence of processing: skulls were split to remove the brains, and long bones were split for marrow. Some bones required little alteration, like a pig fibula which was already pin-shaped, or a horse metapodial which could be simply transformed into an ice-skate. Bone workers did, however, invest considerable time and skill in producing fine objects, like the fourteenth-century knife handle carved in the form of a satyr, from the High Street in Perth (56). At this time most cattle, sheep and goats were horned, and there was a big demand for this product, especially as spoons and cups. Horn does not survive well, but the discarded horn cores do, and sites in Perth have produced vast quantities: 1753 cattle horns and 722 goat from one site alone! Antler was even more elastic and was cut longitudinally into plates, especially for making combs.

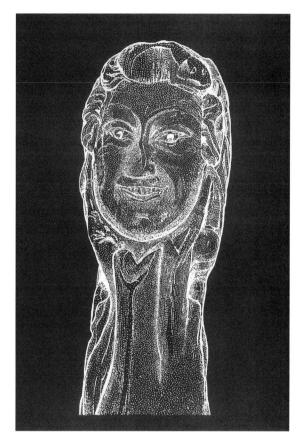

56 *Satyr's head knife handle from Perth.*

A tannery in St Andrews

Not all hides were destined for export as there was a big market for leather which was made into shoes, clothing, belts, scabbards and armour by cobblers and cordwainers. The excavations on the High Street in Perth produced some 6000 pieces, mainly offcuts, of worked leather; not surprising considering that the site was located close to the Skinnergate – 'the street of the leatherworkers'. Part of a tannery was excavated on the northern edge of St Andrews, close to the castle and the sea (57). The site was probably only available for a fairly short time in the fourteenth century while the castle was in ruins. The site consisted of a series of large pits, which were covered by a large, open-sided shed. This was c. 30m (100ft) long and at least 12m (40ft) wide, with the roof supported by large posts. The process involved the removal of the fleshy back layer of the hide by scraping and by steeping in various concoctions of dog dung, oak-bark and urine. Series of pits were required, and those excavated were identified as washing pits by their overflows, which indicated a constant stream of water. These rectangular tanks were between 1m (3ft 4in) and 1.5m (5ft) deep, and were originally timber-lined, with a clay base. Such a shed structure would have been ideal, as finished hides could be left to air-dry from the rafters. As ever, absolute interpretations are problematic when dealing with only partial preservation, and so it is also

57 Reconstruction of fourteenth-century tannery in St Andrews.

possible that this complex was in fact related to the textile industry – maybe for the fulling or dyeing of cloth.

Cereal processing and a mill from medieval Glasgow

Everyone, especially the poor, depended on cereals as their main source of daily calorific intake. The harvest from fields in and around towns and their hinterland, required considerable processing, and the evidence from excavations suggests that the final stages of this were carried out by the miller, in the vicinity of the mill, or else by other consumers. Before milling could be done grain had to be dried in kilns, which were substantial structures, a number of which have been found. Quantities of cereal grains survive

because a fair proportion was accidentally carbonized, both in kilns and during preparation in the home. The kilns were chiefly designed to dry damp corn, enabling threshing, milling or storage. They were built of clay-covered wattle or of stone, and were keyhole-shaped in plan; a fire was set in the passage and the heat drawn through a permeable floor, which consisted of a mat of twigs or horsehair. The cereal was placed on this mat for drying. Kilns were also needed to produce malt for the brewing of ale; this involved first steeping barley in a tank or pit, and then arresting germination by drying in a kiln (58).

Grinding of dried grains to make flour was done both on a domestic scale with handquerns, and on a larger commercial scale in the town mills. The only reasonably complete plan of a mill was found on a site on the eastern outskirts of medieval Glasgow. Excavations at the Saracen's Head Inn found the old Poldrait burn, 3m (10ft) below present ground surface. This had been canalized to form a mill stream, some time before 1500, by creating a narrow, timber-lined channel. A platform was created for the mill on the north side of the

58 Corn drier from North Berwick.

59 *Reconstruction of the Poldrait mill.*

stream. The position of the vertical mill wheel was identified by a depression in the stream bed, which showed that this had been an undershot wheel. One of the original paddles was found in the depression, alongside a stone-built socket for the wheel axle. The mill was built of timber supported by earthfast beams, and measured 10m (33ft) long by 6m (20ft) wide. The access was on the north side, where carts could be backed up to a porched loading bay (59).

Textiles

As we have seen, a large proportion of overseas trade was based on the export of wool, but historical sources also show that the crown was keen to keep enough good-quality wool back for home production, to be less dependent on expensive imported cloth. This helped the economy by providing employment for fullers, dyers and weavers, and also helped the balance of payments.

Two common finds indicate that the preparation of wool and flax was done in many homes, by women of all classes. The first category are teeth from iron heckles, which were a type of comb used to prepare the raw

material for spinning; the second are spindle whorls, used to produce fairly small quantities of yarn by the drop-spinning method. Flax was grown in town and country to make linen; a large number of flax seeds came from the Kirk Close site in Perth. Wooden pin beaters and weaving swords have been found, along with loom weights, which were used with vertical looms, as opposed to the more sophisticated horizontal looms which were in use on the Continent (60, 61). The latter were sure to have been also in use in Scotland, but the evidence suggests that most production here was simple and small scale. This is reinforced by the cloth recovered from excavations, much of which is coarse worsted, white and grey homespun. A number of plants were used to make dyes, and some of the hearths and furnaces which have been found were probably used for heat dyeing in vats. High-quality felted and dyed woollens have also

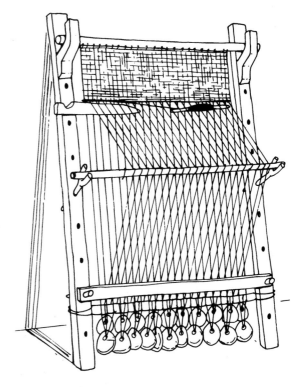

60 *Vertical loom, with weaving to push up warp threads.*

75

61 *Wooden weaving sword from Aberdeen,*

been found, but it has been suggested that these are imports on the whole, as were the silks. The evidence does indicate therefore that the majority of the best wool was exported, so long as there was a market for it.

Metalworking

The winning and smelting of metals took place in the countryside, the unsmithed products being supplied to blacksmiths in the burghs. Smelting was another burgh monopoly, possibly being carried out on a seasonal basis (p. 112). Iron smithing waste is fairly indestructible, and was produced in very large quantities, so is often recovered from urban excavations.

A few well-preserved smithies have been found, and one of the best of these was in Edinburgh Castle, in an area sufficiently re-mote from the principal structures not to be a fire hazard or a smelly nuisance (**62**). A series of smithies existed here from the thirteenth to the sixteenth century, although in the limited area investigated most of the evidence consisted of ground-level hearths, full of smithing debris. A major campaign of repair and building works was instigated by David II in the middle of the fourteenth century, and so

a larger smithy may have been built to supply the demand for ironwork. This can equally be interpreted as an armourer's workshop, which would always have been needed here and at other royal castles. The smithy was within a large rectangular timber shed, which was 8m (26ft) north–south. It was equipped with a stone-built furnace which stood to waist-level, where the fire-grate rested. Part of this was found collapsed into the hollow base, which had to be kept raked-out and free of ashes to allow a free draw of air from the bellows. A post-hole close to the furnace would have supported part of a chimney canopy. No trace was found of a setting for the anvil, but this is not surprising as it probably stood on a tree trunk. Next to the furnace was a quenching trough cut into the bedrock, beside which was a most unusual feature – a hole had been dug in the floor west of the furnace, just big enough to hold a sturdy oak box. The box had a beaten, thin sheet-iron lining which was only 2–3mm thick. It seems to have func-tioned as a cool, clean space where steeled or tempered objects could be allowed to cool gradually (**63**). The partly cobbled floor was strewn with coal, charcoal and smithing debris, including bits of short iron rods. The latter were used to

62 *Reconstruction of Edinburgh Castle and the smithy in the fourteenth century.*

~EDINBURGH CASTLE~

63 *Edinburgh Castle smithy looking north, quenching trough (centre) with furnace base (right) and iron-lined box (left).*

make carpentry nails which were a common product of any medieval smithy. In addition to this debris, a large number of iron artefacts were recovered, including knife blades, an armour-piercing crossbow bolt, buckles, teeth from heckles for combing wool, and horseshoes, along with an array of structural and household hardware. Among these were a few tools which were probably used by the smith, notably a file and a punch.

Historical records tell that the blacksmiths of Perth were concentrated close to the western bounds of the burgh, and sure enough a smithing complex has been uncovered in such a location on Meal Vennel. This dates from the end of the fifteenth century and was in use for about one hundred years. A number of large furnace bases were found here, along with a socketed setting for an anvil or bellows.

Fine metalworking was also an important

burgh industry, and one such workshop was found, of late twelfth-century date, fronting the High Street on the King Edward Street site. Considering that this was a frontage, the workshop building was more akin to the wattle houses found in the backlands. It contained hearths which had been used for bronzeworking. Clay moulds, crucibles, sheet bronze and finished objects are common finds on urban sites, indicating that non-ferrous smithing was abundant. There seem to have been plenty of bronze and brass available for these specialist workers to melt down to make new castings, and to carry out repairs to vessels using sheet bronze. It is possible to differentiate between moulds for making decorative fittings and jewellery, as opposed to moulds for vessels, such as cauldrons, ewers and bowls. Bell moulds have also been found. Excavations on the south side of the High Street in Perth uncovered two halves of a mould made from soapstone, and dated to the fourteenth century. This was designed to produce five finger-rings in a single casting (**colour plate 10**).

Pottery

Pottery is often the best-preserved, most plentiful and one of the most attractive finds on an excavation. As a result archaeologists sometimes attach too much importance to this material, and try to wring too much information from what was after all but one of many types of everyday objects. Vessels of wood, leather, glass and metal were also being used for similar purposes in the home, but do not survive so well (**colour plate 11**).

Ceramic vessels were widely used in the kitchen and on the table, with vigorous local industries known on the east coast, at least, from the twelfth century on. Unfortunately very few kiln sites have been located and excavated, a rare example being at Colstoun in East Lothian. It is very useful to be able to recognize where pots were made, and there-

64 *Medieval pottery vessels from excavations: 1 Low Countries pitcher; 2 Aberdeen redware jug; 3 white gritty-ware cooking pot; 4 Scarborough face-mask jug; 5 Rouen jug; 6 Sieburg stoneware jug; 7, 8, 9 Aberdeen cooking pot, urinal and jar; 10 Raeren stoneware mug; 11 money box; 12 Paffrath ladle (Rhineland); 13 Valencian lustreware dish (Spain); 14 Low Countries skillet.*

fore how far they travelled. This helps identify networks of trade and contact. The most common pottery type, known as white gritty ware, was being produced from the twelfth century on in Fife, Lothian and the Borders. An important, well-dated group of locally made glazed jugs, and plain, straight-sided cooking pots, was found in a pit beneath the infirmary hall at Kelso Abbey (p. 16). The suggestion was made here that the technology to produce these wheel-thrown, well-fired products, may have been introduced and spread by the incoming Tironensian monks. This restricted range of products was added to by globular cooking pots and storage jars. In Perth and other areas to the north of the Tay, the local industry produced redwares, so named because of the local iron-rich clays,

which on firing turned this distinctive colour. Production of white gritty ware lasted for about 300 years, and this ware proved to be very popular, turning up on sites throughout Scotland (**64**).

Cooking pots were used for heating food, with the pot being placed directly on the edge of a fire, resulting in smoke-blackening of the base and sides. From the fourteenth century on there seems to have been little demand for cooking pots, possibly because of the availability of metal pots which performed much better. The demand for green-glazed jugs was high, and efforts were made to copy the ornate decoration of vessels produced in Scarborough, and imported into Scotland in considerable numbers. Human face masks were a common decorative form. Local potters were also making oil lamps and curfews – a ceramic cover placed over the fire at night, acting as a kind of storage heater. Food-storage jars of various sizes, some very large, have been found. Jars found in the Paisley Abbey drain (p. 28) had internal lips on the rim where a lid sat, with evidence of a wax seal.

Considerable study has been made of the sherds of imported pottery found on excavations, although this usually represents only 1–3 per cent of the total assemblage. Vessels were coming in from England, France, the Low Countries, Germany and Spain, and these were often attractive, high-quality pieces. An argument has been expressed that these pots were not traded themselves, but rather appear as an adjunct to trade in other commodities, or because they were containers for traded goods. It does seem more likely, however, that most of the imported pots were trade items, especially when considering the greater quantities of French and Spanish wares which have been recorded from sites on the west coast. This may suggest that there was more direct trade between the west of Scotland and those countries, whereas the east-coast burghs were looking more across the North Sea and the Baltic.

The interpretation of pottery from excavations is problematic, not least because so much is recovered from middens, rather than from well-sealed pits. The nature of surface middens is that these were regularly turned over, or otherwise interfered with, and therefore the pottery is rarely in a sound, datable context. This situation is further aggravated by the general lack of typological development seen in the local products, so that a jug from the thirteenth century may not be characteristically different to a jug of fifteenth-century date.

65 *Yellow Spanish silk with dove design from Perth, thirteenth century.*

Personal possessions from the High Street, Perth excavations

This site has produced by far the most complete range of personal objects, and is a useful case-study. Many of the objects are purely functional, while others suggest efforts to express style and individuality through decoration and adornment. Artefacts are of course most useful in attempting an understanding of the status of the people who lived in the buildings in question. It has been suggested that this site was exceptional, especially in the twelfth and thirteenth centuries, because of its richness and range of luxury objects. The counter to this argument is that this was generally a boom time in the burghs, and as ever we do have a tendency to diminish the sophistication of the medieval population from our late twentieth-century perspective. So in fact the only really exceptional aspects of this site were the large scale of excavation, linked to the remarkable quality of preservation.

No complete items of clothing survived, but over 300 fragments were recovered, and around 25 per cent of the woollen items were dyed, mainly red and yellow. Wealthier women could obtain fine imported textiles, such as hair-nets, including one dated to *c*. 1300, which had a cross and crosslet design. In addition there were cultivated silks, imported from the Mediterranean or further afield. One of the most beautiful silks was not found here, but came from the Kirk Close backland site across the High Street. This featured a repeating design of opposed pairs of doves, separated by a narrow vertical band. This exquisite silk was golden yellow in colour, and had been imported from Spain in the thirteenth century to adorn the dress of a burgess's wife (**65**).

Lots of clothing-fasteners were found, including pins, brooches, buttons and buckles (**66**). Most of the latter were used with leather belts and straps, and leather was also very

66 A lead 'spangle' with animal decoration – a thirteenth-century decorative badge that would have been sewn on to clothing.

important for use in clothing and of course footwear. Leatherworkers' tools were found here, on a site which charted over 400 years of footwear fashion, showing that styles changed quite regularly (**67**). Most footwear were low ankle boots of turnshoe construction, meaning that they were made inside out, and when finished were turned right-way around with the grain on the outside (**colour plate 12**). Lots of worn soles were discarded while the uppers were reused. Cold and muddy conditions were attested by the discovery of shoe accessories, including a wooden patten for a child's shoe, which raised the wearer up while walking through mud (**68**). A number of plain and decorated knife sheaths were also found (**69**).

Arms and armour were everyday items, and this site produced a battle-axe, a spearhead, seven iron arrowheads, and part of the handle

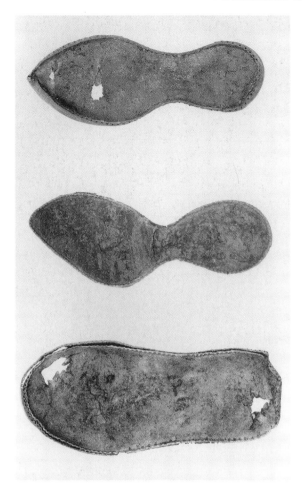

67 Soles from twelfth-century shoes.

68 Wooden patten for a child's shoe.

of a twelfth-century sword. Chainmail was found within a thirteenth-century aisled hall, and a number of spurs were recovered including one decorated with an animal head (**70**). These were the possessions of high-status individuals; such important people were recording transactions in documents, which could only be validated by their seal. One such seal was found, which had belonged to a William Brown, who lived during the thirteenth century.

Medieval towns contained numerous pits and ditches, and so it was not unexpected to find the iron blades from wooden spades. Scythe blades stress the importance of agriculture within and without the burgh, and shears found here could equally have been used for cutting cloth as for shearing sheep. To contrast with these workaday tools, the more esoteric aspects of everyday life were represented by a variety of finds, most eloquently expressed in the discovery of part of a wooden harp, carved with an animal-head terminal (**71**).

Christian faith and pilgrimage were also well represented: a rosary and crucifix made from Whitby jet were found, along with souvenirs of pilgrimages to the great shrines at Canterbury, Walsingham and St Andrews.

Food and drink

The staple diet of porridge, broth, bread and ale is attested in the environmental samples from urban excavations as oats, barley and rye. Ale was the everyday drink, from breakfast to supper, being a weak barley beer. Indeed it has been suggested that as much as a third of the barley crop was destined for brewing! Wheat was also available for the merchants, nobles and clerics, although at times this could only be obtained as an expensive import. A number of bread ovens have been excavated, most of which are small, domestic types, found outdoors in backlands, consisting of a circular hearthstone covered by a wattle-and-clay dome. A commercial-scale

69 *Decorated leather belt or strap, fourteenth century.*

baxter's (baker's) oven was found at Kirk Close, Perth. This was a 2m (6ft 7in) long structure, with a lower fire chamber, allowing heating to be continuous (p. 60).

The choice of vegetables was limited, and are chiefly represented by kail, a form of cabbage which was chopped and stewed. Peas and beans were available, but sometimes only as an import. Wild fruits and nuts are often found, and these were collected on an opportunistic, seasonal basis from the hinterland by the townsfolk. These include: cherries, apples, brambles, raspberries, blueberries, elderberries, rowans and hazelnuts.

Meat was available, but whether it was always affordable to the mass of the population is another matter. It was cooked by boiling or roasting. Beef seems to have been the most frequently eaten, which is not surprising as cattle produced the greatest weight of meat. Next in popularity was sheep, followed by pig, goat, horse and deer. A butcher's shop has never been found, but the bone assemblages exhibit ample evidence of butchery in the form of chop and saw marks. Sometimes only the poorer meat-bearing extremity bones are found, possibly indicating that the consumers were poor, or that only these cuts were available, while the best haunches went for preserving. Meat was

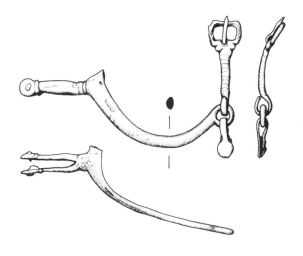

70 *Rowel-spur, fourteenth century.*

71 *Animal-head terminal from a stringed instrument (harp?), thirteenth century.*

bought fresh from the market and either hung for immediate use, or else preserved by salting or pickling in a sealed barrel. Another alternative was smoking which could be done in the home, with smaller joints of mutton or pork hung over the fire. Domestic chickens and geese were also popular, as were the occasional wild geese, curlews and seagulls. Venison was not an important part of the diet, and even in burghs which were close to major forests, for example Aberdeen, red and roe deer accounted for only 1–2 per cent of the food-forming animals. This may simply mean that it was jealously kept for the tables of the noble forest proprietors. Sheep and goats' milk were important for the manufacture of butter and cheese; cattle kept their milk for the raising of calves.

Tiny fragments of figs, grapes and walnuts, which originated in the eastern Mediterranean and Middle East, have been found as food debris in cesspits. These were only available to the better off, as were the imported spices, which added zest to otherwise lacklustre fare, with the added advantage of hiding the flavour of rancid or badly preserved meat.

The fishing industry formed an important part of the food economy; and fish is represented in the archaeological record as being a major part of the diet, and in the documentary record as an important element of the export trade. Fresh and preserved fish were eaten in towns, depending on the season. There is a bias in the retrieval of fishbones on excavations in favour of the larger bones of marine species, dominated by cod, and followed by ling, saithe, haddock, plaice and halibut. These were caught at sea with handlines, whereas nets were used for catching smaller fish, especially herring. River and estuarine fish are represented, notably salmon and eels, which were caught with traps and nets.

Health and death

We can get literally under the skin of the townspeople themselves by examining their skeletal remains, which are the only real source of evidence we have to provide some understanding of life-style and health. In recent years over 2000 individuals have been excavated, and common patterns have emerged for the medieval population throughout the length and breadth of the country. Also of interest is the fact that these trends did not change significantly during this 500-year period. Not surprisingly, the overall picture is one of short, hard lives. On average, men lived longer than women, unlike today.

Hard times affected children most of all, and this is reflected both in high levels of infant mortality and also in the regular occurrence of markers of childhood 'morbidity' – illness and malnutrition – seen in those who survived. Although many recovered, this left a detectable legacy of arrested growth and ill health often resulting in death in young adulthood. Evidence of healthcare is rare but can be detected; the clearest signs of medical intervention being the setting of bone fractures and trepanation. The latter refers to the drilling of a hole in the skull to relieve pressure, this operation often being the actual cause of death! Tooth extraction was probably common, although the only good example is from Soutra Hospital. Dental health was generally poor; the coarse diet helped remove plaque, but at the same time the fine grits in flour ground by stone querns wore away enamel, resulting in abscesses and gum disease.

Wounding in battle was an occupational hazard for many, and no doubt attempts were made to treat these. Some healed sword-cuts on skulls have certainly been observed. The most notable life-style indicators, however, are the many instances of damage to bones caused by repeated exertions. Vertical stress on the body is common, caused by lifting heavy loads, and is seen in both men and women. At Whithorn, the population was examined for enthesopathies, which are bony growths on muscle attachments resulting from muscles pulling on the bone. This examination identified a gender difference: men were exerting their lower limbs, while women were doing something powerful with their upper limbs. Occasionally a skeleton will provide a real insight, such as one young man from Whithorn who had a very robust torso, but withered lower limbs with bony growths on his hands: the interpretation being that he was crippled and had to propel himself along with his hands.

Acute infection has been identified as the most common cause of death, although recognizing this is difficult. So much acute illness would have led to sudden death, before the illness could leave its mark on the bones. Tuberculosis has been recognized, since it leaves lesions on the spine and on the ribs. A case of healed TB was seen in one child who died aged about nine, found in the Carmelite friary cemetery in Aberdeen. Although healed, the TB caused the vertebrae to collapse, leaving the child paralysed from the waist down (**72**). Syphilis and leprosy were probably common, although no leper cemetery has ever been excavated. Pilgrims were often seeking a miraculous cure from chronic illness or congenital abnormalities, and it is reasonable to suggest that many died and were buried at their goal. The shrine of St Ninian at Whithorn was a popular medieval pilgrimage site, but surprisingly the cemetery was found to contain the remains of a fairly representative Scottish medieval assemblage.

Some useful data on life expectancy has

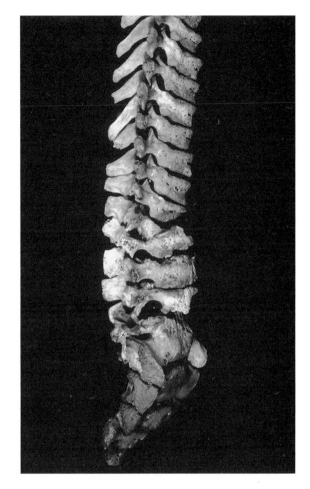

72 *Lower vertebral column from an eight–ten-year-old child, showing effects of healed tuberculosis. From the Carmelites' cemetery, Aberdeen.*

been provided from the excavated populations from Aberdeen and Linlithgow. Of the 207 individuals from the latter site, 58 per cent died before they were eighteen years old, while in Aberdeen this figure was 33 per cent. Half of all of these died before they reached their sixth birthday. Less than 25 per cent of the adults reached middle age, and very few achieved old age.

CHAPTER SIX

Earthwork castles

In the twelfth century the crown sought to extend and consolidate royal control by granting estates to native and foreign feudal lords, the latter being chiefly Anglo-Normans, Bretons and Flemings. These lords, and existing Celtic magnates, needed to provide themselves with defensive and residential bases which were quick and cheap to build, while still reflecting their superiority. Earthwork castles were ideal for this purpose, an extreme example being the motte at Dover, reputedly built for William the Conqueror in only five days. Moreover, the Scottish countryside was littered with glacial mounds which were easily converted into mottes. So we can see that the landscape influenced the siting, form and popularity of such castles during the primary phase of colonization, and beyond.

As many as 300 or so earthwork castles have been recorded, although only a handful of these have been excavated. The largest concentrations are in the north-east and in the south-west, both of which were areas that were traditionally independent, and here the distribution of earthwork castles charts the advance of royal control by means of military campaigns. By analysing the distribution of such sites we can identify communication routes and frameworks of power in the countryside. Such castles can be loosely grouped as ringworks, mottes and moated sites, although there are many more variations of form within Scotland. These small castles of

earth, turf and timber probably originated in Normandy in the eleventh century, and were introduced into Scotland by the new breed of feudal lords.

Defences

In building an earthwork castle, one of the first activities was to dig defensive ditches which not only provided an immediate barrier, but also produced large amounts of material which could instantly be used to throw up ramparts and to elevate natural mounds. Where outer bailey enclosures existed, these would also be encircled by a ditch. Baileys were separated from the motte by inner ditches, as seen at Auldhill, Portencross (Ayrshire), where a double ditch was found. Excavations have uncovered two phases of pre-medieval occupation, which is not surprising on this site which has a commanding view of the Firth of Clyde. This was a stronghold of the de Ros family, who converted this natural motte-and-bailey shape into a castle in the twelfth century. Here and at Cruggleton (Wigtown), existing ancient fortifications were adapted. Cruggleton is on a clifftop on the east side of the Whithorn peninsula, and the promontory is cut off by a wide ditch enclosing a bailey 135m (443ft) north–south by 45m (150ft) wide. The castle itself was on an inner promontory also isolated by a ditch. This was a seat of the early lords of Galloway, and the

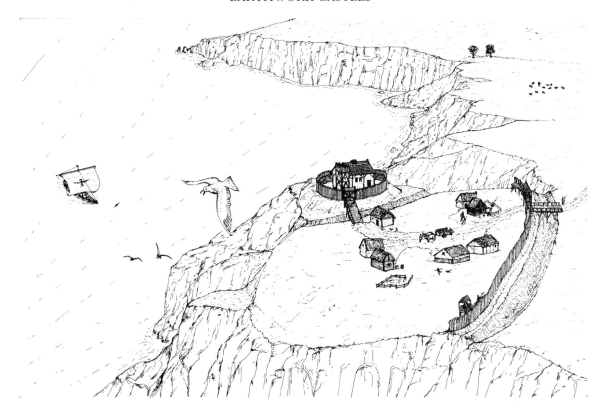

73 *Reconstruction of Cruggleton in the twelfth century.*

defences of this site were probably strengthened during the troubles of the 1170s and 1180s between Roland of Galloway and royal forces. At this time the summit was transformed into a 25m (83ft) wide defensive platform (**73**).

Banks outside ditches, known as counterscarp banks, were also seen, a good example being at Lumphanan (Aberdeenshire). Here a large area was lowered between the base of the mound and the site of the outer bank, creating a marshy hollow. Many inland sites were located on water courses which were often incorporated into their defences along with any areas of boggy ground. This is seen particularly well at Castlehill of Strachan (Kincardine), the construction of which has been dated by excavation to *c.* 1250, when it is known to have been in the hands of the Giffards. At that time the site was effectively

an island surrounded by streams and bog which formed a natural outer enclosure beyond the motte, which needed no additional defences to protect any outbuildings such as the stores, kitchens and byres which may have existed here. This is a natural glacial mound of compacted sands and gravels, which had a tail running away from it to the south forming a raised causeway. The east side of the mound was washed by a stream which was incorporated into the defences (**74**).

Castle of Wardhouse (Aberdeenshire) is one of the few moated sites ever investigated. Historical evidence tells us that this was a castle with a chapel, which had been built by 1230 for a man called Bartholomew the Fleming. This was constructed on a natural platform jutting out from a hillside, and excavations have shown that this was provided with double ditches and earth ramparts. The inner rampart, which was 8.6m (29ft) wide, enclosed a large flat platform where the castle buildings stood.

74 *The motte at Strachan, isolated by medieval water courses.*

The bishops of Glasgow provided themselves with an earthwork castle in the twelfth century; excavations have shown that by 1200 this consisted of a 28m (92ft) diameter ringwork, which dominated the west front of the cathedral. This was only 50m (165ft) away from the ringwork, which was built on the main axis of the great church. The ringwork had been formed by digging a large, circular ditch, which was regularly cleaned so as not to compromise its defensive capability. A timber bridge and gatehouse had been constructed to allow access over the north-east part of the ditch. The bishops would have had a fine timber hall, chambers and ancillary buildings within the ringwork, but none of the primary structures survived to be excavated.

Turf was an important building material, and was used in the construction of a number of mottes to help consolidate the heaped-up, loose gravels. At Strachan turf was used to help stitch together dumps of gravel at the summit edges, to create a 20m (67ft) diameter platform. Material from digging ditches and from scarping sides was piled up on the top, sometimes doubling the height of the natural mound as in the case of Lumphanan. This castle of the powerful Durward family was constructed in the mid-thirteenth century, and was provided with a shoulder bank of turf with a possible palisade, further strengthened by a stone revetment found just below the shoulder. A motte formed the focus of one of the early forms of the great medieval fortress at Dundonald (Ayrshire). The motte was probably constructed *c*. 1161 by Walter Fitzalan, who had been Steward to David I. When Walter first came to the site, the ancient fortification enclosing the hilltop would have resembled a ringwork, and it was a logical progression to add a motte to this which extended the defensive circuit and overlooked the natural line of approach. The motte had a basal diameter of 25m (83ft) and was constructed on a raft of boulders and clay. A stone revetment was added to the base of the motte possibly in the thirteenth century, at a time when the coast was in danger of attack from the Norse. Such a revetment has also been found at Strachan, making access up the steep side of the motte more difficult for attackers, while at the same time strengthening the structure of the mound.

Most mottes would have a single entrance at the summit, access to which was by way of a timber bridge, known as a flying bridge, or else by a cobbled path running around the side of the mound. A good example of the latter was found during excavations at Lumphanan, although this may have been secondary and could have been preceded by a flying bridge (75). A rare entrance structure was found at Portencross, which consisted of a tower formed from three sets of twinned post-pits, which would have supported a pair of heavy doors. Such an entrance tower was probably a standard feature, allowing any raised walkway behind the palisade to continue over the entrance. A palisade of large timber posts, with or without an earth bank, is almost always found on the edge of a motte summit during excavations. These have already been mentioned as existing at Lumphanan and Portencross, and one was also found during excavations at Rattray (Buchan). The latter motte was built *c.* 1200, formed from a natural oval-shaped, sand-dune overlooking a good natural harbour on the coast. The summit was 35m (115ft) wide, and was enclosed by an insubstantial rampart, revetted with clay and stone. A village and parish church were established around the motte during the thirteenth century.

75 *Lumphanan motte and cobbled path.*

In Scotland the term 'motte' is used very broadly, and in many cases is just a convenient term which covers a multitude of variations. This is certainly true at Cruggleton where the motte summit was only 3.25m (11ft) higher than the bailey, and formed by dumping earth to the west and north of a pre-existing defended platform. This was later transformed into a complex stone castle, thus obliterating much of the earlier buildings. Many other mottes, however, were never rebuilt in stone; such artificial mounds being inherently unstable. In such cases the summit palisade can survive to be discovered by excavation.

A common form of palisade was created around the summit by digging large post-pits at roughly 3m (10ft) centres. This was found to be the case at Roberton (Lanark), a motte built on the banks of the Clyde during the Wars of Independence in the early fourteenth century. The primary palisade at Strachan was also of the same design, the space between the individual posts being infilled either with horizontal planks or with turf. This palisade may only have stood for about twenty years, when some of the posts started to slip down the loose edge of the motte. This prompted the Giffards to extend the summit by dumping more layers of gravel, into which a new palisade was constructed. This was formed from tightly spaced, stone-packed post settings enclosing a summit which was now over 20m (67ft) in diameter. The new palisade was formed from timbers 200–300mm (8–12in) square, at 500mm (20in) centres. Features inside the palisade hinted at the existence of a continuous wall-walk or else one or more flimsy watch-towers. Good evidence of such a fighting-platform was found at Portencross, in the form of an inner ring of posts inside the palisade.

Almost all palisades enclose an oval or circular area, an exception being the summit lip defences at Barton Hill, Kinnaird (Perthshire). The rocky sides of this volcanic plug had been scarped to form a steep-sided motte sometime in the late twelfth century, probably with a bailey to the south-west. On excavation this castle was found to have been provided with a sharply angled summit defence, which created a 15m (50ft) wide, rectangular enclosure. This consisted of a dry-stone wall base, which formed a revetment to a bank of turf and timber. It is uncertain as to whether this was a primary feature, or a later addition made before the site was abandoned in the fourteenth century.

At Kinnaird, a double square of post-pits can be interpreted as a small timber tower, 4m (13ft) wide, enclosed by a snugly fitting stockade, with only a narrow space between the two. This was probably a stilted watch-tower which was erected within the southern angle of the outer summit enclosure. A slightly larger square tower was found at Keir Knowe of Drum (Stirling), built on nine large posts.

Timber halls

Only three of the sites featured above have produced substantial remains of hall buildings on motte summits, in addition to which only at Dundonald have bailey structures been found. Here, a Dark Age building platform was adapted as the base for a small hall, aligned north to south, 5.3m (17ft) in length. A stone ramp was added to allow access to the hall from the east. This building was replaced and overlapped by a larger hall, built with posts held in low stone walls. This contained a hearth and had earth floors. Like so many halls it was divided by a partition into two rooms, essentially a public room (for business and dining) and a private chamber (withdrawing and/or bedroom); this arrangement is usually described as a 'hall and solar'. These buildings at Dundonald were in use for a period of almost one hundred years, and would have stood with others until the time of a major rebuilding in the 1240s. They may well have been of secondary importance to any hall or tower which stood on the motte.

The rectangular timber hall found on the motte summit at Cruggleton is something of an oddity; at Dundonald a principal bailey hall was built on the site of a long-demolished house, whereas at Cruggleton, Roland of Galloway seems to have deliberately chosen to incorporate and extend a Dark Age hall which had already stood on this site in some form for about 400 years. It may be that the very timbers were imbued with a tradition of lordship which he wished to be seen as perpetuating, and so instead of building afresh he simply doubled the length of the old hall to create a 12m (40ft) long hall (**76**). The construction technique was of main timbers held in pits, with infill wattle walls. A fairly sophisticated plan was created, with a small tower added at the north-west corner, built on four posts. This complex, which was probably in use until the late thirteenth century, is paralleled at Lismahon in Co. Down, a part of Ireland closely connected to south-west Scotland at this time by culture and politics.

Part of the royal earthwork castle has been excavated at Peebles, which was built by *c.*

76 *Post-pits for the twelfth-century hall at Cruggleton.*

1150. Partial excavation of the summit revealed two substantial timber buildings, one of which was a circular hall (or maybe even a tower), built with a ring of vertical timbers set within a shallow trench. This had a diameter of *c.* 12m (40ft), with part of the weight of the roof taken on external 'corner' posts. The other building was 5.5m (18ft) in length and designed so that the interior roof supports divided the ground-plan into three bays. This had a disproportionately large entrance, and was some kind of service building, possibly a stable.

The only other circular medieval timber building was found on the summit of the motte at Strachan (**77**). This was definitely a single-storey hall, which occupied more than 50 per cent of the summit. The hall was *c.* 11m (37ft) in diameter, and the height to the apex of the roof would have been *c.* 8m (27ft), with the overall appearance very much like that of an Iron Age roundhouse. It was framed on a ring of large posts, the ghosts of which could still be seen in some of the post-pits. These posts would have supported rafters which met at the roof apex, with additional strength provided by cross-beams between opposed pairs of rafters. The roof was probably of thatch lain on wattle panels. Wall remains were represented by large quantities of baked daub, found with wattle impressions. A hall and solar arrangement is suggested by the internal planning, which meant that the space was always divided into two by a partition, with one large room, and a small room initially at the north end. The Strachan hall covered an area of 110sq m (361sq ft), which is half as much again as the smarter burgesses' houses excavated on the High Street site in Perth, and about four times as big as the average area occupied by small backland buildings in Aberdeen.

The area between the hall and the palisade contained large amounts of midden debris, and more was found tipped down the edges and in the ditch. A group of three furnaces

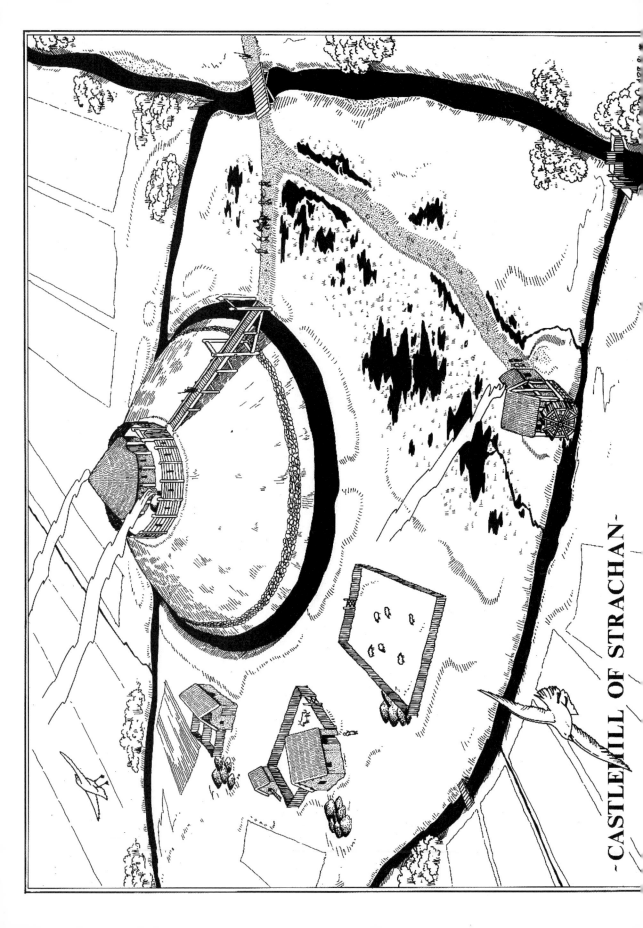

~CASTLEHILL OF STRACHAN~

were found in the north summit area, each one having been based with a single, reused granite millstone, 1m (3ft 4in) in diameter (**78**). The furnaces would have supported vats used either for cooking or for brewing, and only one was in use at any time. The mill-stones indicated the presence of the lord's mill nearby on the River Feugh. Each stone was very heavy, and they would not have been moved far once they were worn out. Metal-working was another important activity on the motte, highlighted by the discovery of debris produced in both the refining of blooms, and the production and repair of wrought-iron objects. Various personal belongings were recovered, including bronze and silver cloak-pins, a silver finger-ring, tweezers, knife blades, and a whetstone. Keys from padlocks and from a chest were found. The excavated evidence produced a clear picture of a site which was intensively occupied for about sixty years, before being destroyed by fire. The historical evidence would indicate destruction at the hands of the army of Robert the Bruce in 1308.

The same fate probably befell the timber hall on the motte at Rattray, destroyed at the same time as Strachan. This was during the 'harrying of Buchan', when the earl, John Comyn, forfeited his land for opposing the king. The Comyns had acquired the property shortly after 1210, and immediately altered the motte to increase its domestic importance at the expense of its defensibility. The summit bank and palisade were flattened in part to allow the construction of an aisled hall, an action they may have regretted in 1308!

The hall was 20m (67ft) long and 10m (33ft) wide, and was framed in timber based on clay-bonded, rubble foundations. The roof was probably thatched with a ridge of glazed tiles. The interior was floored in clay and was

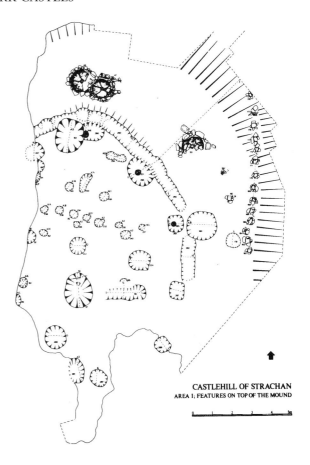

78 Strachan: plan of hall, furnaces and secondary palisade.

divided into three rooms, with a large central space. The stone base for a bench was found at the east end of the main room, with a hearth in front of it. The west room might have been screened off as an entrance vestibule. There was ample space on the summit for other buildings, but none survived.

Stone halls added to earthwork castles

The Comyn lands at Rattray were granted to Archibald Douglas *c.* 1324, and the excavated evidence shows that he quickly set about building a lordly complex of four or more stone structures atop the motte. At the core of these was a hall, built on a grand scale, 23m

77 Reconstruction of Strachan in the late thirteenth century with mill and causeway.

93

(78ft) in length. This had clay-bonded walls, with simple, mortared architectural mouldings for doors and windows, which were probably glazed. Thatch was still used for the roof of this single-storey building. Another feature shared with the earlier timber hall was the subdivision of the interior into three rooms, this time with a pair of opposing benches, one midway along each of the long walls of the largest middle room (**colour plate 13**).

The hall had a rectangular, stone-built kitchen to the north, and an almost square ancillary structure to the west. The summit was covered in middens, and was muddy, with cobbled paths which linked individual buildings with each other and with the entrance. Around the buildings were a large group of furnaces and ovens, some of which were close to the west entrance into the likely kitchen block. Only a small number of the ovens were in use contemporaneously, as they were cut one into another. These were almost exclusively domestic and were similar to those found at Strachan. Some were the bases for heating-vats, whereas others here were certainly bread ovens.

The animal-bone assemblage from Rattray confirms the obvious suggestion that such sites served as bases for hunting, the favourite pursuit of the medieval nobility. Bones of red, roe and fallow deer were found, along with remains of wild boar, hare, rabbit and wolf. A hunting reserve is known to have existed to the west of Rattray, which may have contained areas of dense forest, sheltering wild boar. Artefacts of the hunt were found at the castle, in the form of arrowheads and a ceramic hunting-horn. The finds indicated the wealth of the occupants, including a fine silver-gilt brooch, decorated with four leopard heads and dated to the fourteenth century (**79**). The archaeological and historical evidence combine to show that this lordly complex stood on the motte for between 100 and 150 years, before being abandoned in the late fifteenth century.

Excavations at the Bishop's Castle in Glasgow have revealed another case where a stone hall was added to an earlier earthwork castle, compromising its defensibility to some extent. Excavations on the ringwork at the front of the cathedral showed that a 15m (50ft) long rectangular hall was added to the site in the late thirteenth century, with its west wall built in the bottom of the ditch. Not surprisingly the corners had to be clasped with buttresses. The old timber gatehouse was probably replaced in stone at the same time. These structures stood for about one hundred years at which time they were levelled, and replaced by a substantial tower house, with a chamfered base of good-quality ashlar.

Observations on earthwork castles

From the twelfth century on, these sites provided a framework for the pacification and administration of large areas within the developing kingdom. Excavation results indicate that considerable imagination and flexibility were applied by the builders, the designs

79 *Silver brooch from Rattray.*

94

often being governed by topography and the availability of building materials. Ancient sites were utilized, as well as fresh ones, and local building traditions influenced the end result. There were probably as many different designs as there were mottes, ringworks and moated sites: forms of defence which adapted well to both urban and rural locations. They were built for kings, barons, lords and churchmen, often occupied on their behalf by officials and officers. Many were on estates which were the minor possessions of great lords. Their construction and occupation spanned a long period, probably longer than anywhere else in Europe, with some being built anew in response to the militarization of the years on either side of 1300 and beyond.

In most cases, an outer enclosure would have existed, although these rarely survive. Here were placed some of the ancillary and industrial structures, which together with the lord's hall or tower would comprise what can best be described as a 'manor', the term being used here to mean the principal dwelling-house of an estate. In many cases they were fitted into an existing rural settlement pattern, while others acted as a catalyst for settlement, for example at Rattray. As manorial centres they would have provided employment for a household, along with craftsmen and metalworkers. They were places of consumption and redistribution of produce and livestock, paid as rents by feudal tenants, who had no choice but to use the lord's mill, which was often located close to the castle.

Earthwork castles were multi-functional, serving as manor houses, monastic granges, hunting-lodges, strategic garrisoned forts, and especially as seats of local government and justice. Excavations have shown how the occupants pursued domestic comfort: the spacious halls and multiple ovens conjuring up images of pleasurable feasting on the fruits of field and forest. The other side of this coin being the signs of violent destruction of earthwork castles during the Wars of Independence, many of which were never occupied again, their functions being replaced by the stone tower houses later built for the same clientele.

CHAPTER SEVEN

Castles in context

The stark ruins of Scotland's stone castles have been subjected to extensive architectural dissection, which tells us little about the people who constructed and lived in these buildings. Even more importantly, archaeology has shown that the standing remains often represent only half of the total accommodation, negating the results of any functional analysis based only on the evidence of what has survived as an accident of history. Carefully designed excavations have revealed a complex developmental story; the results showing that towers and keeps were not free-standing and self-contained, but depended rather on other enclosed ranges of buildings, which have long disappeared from view.

This is not an attempt to retell the fascinating history of the Scottish castle, but rather to show how archaeology is enriching and advancing our understanding. We have already seen how many castles were damaged during the Wars of Independence, including the stone castles of enclosure which were built in the thirteenth century. In these the emphasis was placed on mural towers, sometimes thrusting aggressively out from the walls, stressing the military rather than the residential. When these came to be rebuilt in the later fourteenth century the favoured form was that of the tower or hall house, an increasingly residential form which persisted until the end of our period and beyond. The influence of artillery on siege warfare is apparent by the

mid-fifteenth century, and one hundred years later was so great that entirely new designs of artillery fortifications were introduced.

Portencross

Excavations have shown that the de Ros lords rebuilt their timber castle at Portencross (Ayrshire) in the late thirteenth century, by raising and extending the natural motte platform, with layers of stone infilling the bedrock to a thickness of 2.5m (8ft). This created a base for building a rectangular stone-walled enclosure, which measured 17m (56ft) by 12m (40ft). This is difficult to interpret and could either have been roofed as a hall house, or else left open as a small enclosure castle, with buildings pent against the walls. The entrance was in the thickened west wall facing into the bailey, and close to this, at the north-west corner, was a small latrine tower.

Whatever the original design of the stone castle was, this was radically altered c. 1300 when a timber hall, constructed on stone footings, was built inside the walls. A few years later this was extended to its full size, which was 10m (33ft) in length, occupying most of the enclosed space. A single entrance in the middle of the south wall gave access into the hall, which had an earth floor and a central fireplace. The roof would have been covered with turf or thatch on a backing of planks. The hall was the lord's residence, with other accommodation and service buildings being located in the bailey to the west. The reconstruction drawing (**80**) shows how the de Ros castle would have looked before they forfeited this and their other possessions *c.* 1315, having opposed Robert I. The site was then held by the Boyds until they built a stone tower house nearby.

Cruggleton

At about the same time as Portencross was rebuilt in stone, so Alexander Comyn, the Earl of Buchan, transformed and strengthened Cruggleton (Wigtown), to create a curtain-walled fortress with a central tower. This building campaign was probably still under-way in 1292, when he applied to Edward I of England for permission to roof the eight turrets of his castle. A massive, four-tiered and

80 *Portencross; reconstruction of the castle c. 1300.*

stepped foundation of clay and boulders was built around the base of the motte. This was the raft upon which the stone curtain-wall was built, facing the landward side. Although in some ways unnecessary, the curtain was also extended around the west and south cliff edges, to create a triangular enclosure. This would have been very impressive when approached from the sea. The entrance was in the north part of the circuit, associated with a stone platform which was probably the base of a drawbridge. This could be lowered over the recut ditch which isolated the inner promon-tory from the outer bailey.

Having entered the castle the fourteenth-century visitor was confronted by the main rectangular tower, which was built against the south curtain, replacing the timber tower. The stone tower was found to have originally been 15m (50ft) by 10m (33ft), with two small ground-floor chambers enclosed by massively thick walls. The main entrance to the tower was at first-floor level, presumably reached by

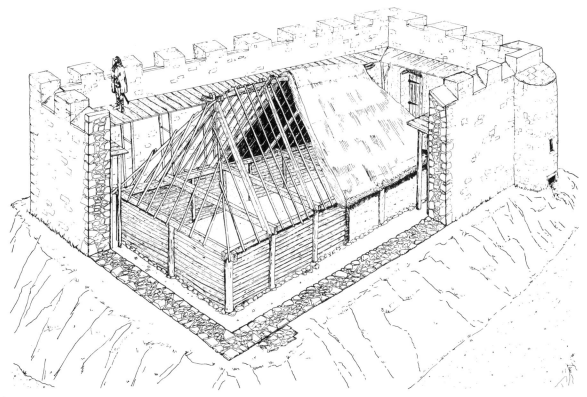

a forestair. Little survived of the primary stone buildings inside the curtain due to severe damage resulting from an attack in 1308 by Edward Bruce, brother of the king. After this the Comyns' castle may have been left in ruins for fifty years or more.

Restoration commenced when Cruggleton came into the ownership of the priors of Whithorn in 1423. The tower was reduced in ground-plan, refaced and heightened, with the main accommodation being provided in a range of buildings against the landward curtain-wall. A single building was found in the angle of the east and south curtains: this contained a large hearth, and was probably the kitchen, placed furthest away from the other buildings because of the fire risk. The entrance was impressively rebuilt with a flanking tower on either side, and a gatehouse which housed the drawbridge mechanism. The east gatehouse tower was best preserved and found to measure 4.5m (15ft) internally, within massively thick walls. This was L-shaped in plan, with a garderobe tower at the back, kept clean by a sluiced drain which flushed the effluent over the cliff (**81**). This castle, like many others in the later medieval period, was adapted to utilize artillery, as seen in the discovery of gun loops of sixteenth-century date.

Dundonald

Dundonald (Ayrshire) stands today as a marvellous example of a late fourteenth-century tower house, built by Robert II, the first of the great Stewart dynasty. Although the castle first appears in historical documents at this time, the excavations revealed prehistoric and early medieval fortifications dating back many centuries earlier. Of great importance were the remains of an earlier stone castle, which seems to be one of the rare concentric enclosure castles in Scotland. This may have been on a par with the Edwardian castles of Wales, and thus was at the forefront of European military engineering.

It seems likely that the concentric castle was constructed between the 1240s and 1280s on the orders of Alexander Stewart, one of the

81 Cruggleton; east gatehouse tower, with base of the garderobe tower (right foreground).

82 Reconstruction of the concentric castle at Dundonald.

chief nobles of the realm (**82**). He had the wealth and vision to execute this advanced design, having been influenced by a visit to the famous northern French castle of Coucy-le-Château during a pilgrimage to Santiago de Compostela. It has long been suggested that Coucy was the inspiration for Kildrummy, Dirleton and Bothwell, which were similar in design to the enclosure castle found at Dundonald. The excavations have shown that the earlier motte and other defences were levelled to create a raised platform which exaggerated the scale of a pair of elongated, D-shaped towers which now formed the east entrance. These towers each had a curved front and steeply angled base, which gave them stability and made them difficult to attack. The south tower contained a well-shaft, probably the main water supply for the castle, and the location of this may have

helped determine the overall plan (**83**). The towers were 11m (37ft) wide, and guarded a 12m (40ft) long entrance passage. These towers were probably mirrored at the west end of the hill by an identical pair, remains of which can be seen incorporated into the later tower house. Just inside the west towers, and facing the main entrance, was a single rectangular stone building, 10m (33ft) in length. This was probably the chapel, and was to be a constant feature of the developing castle over the next 300 years.

The construction programme would have been accelerated *c.* 1260 under the threat of an invasion of the west by Haakon IV of Norway, which culminated in the battle of Largs in 1263 in which the Scots were victorious. Meanwhile, construction at Dundonald continued, possibly with the grandiose plan of a curtain-wall and minor mural towers to north and south, which were never fully completed. The excavations produced evidence of massive destruction,

83 *Dundonald: southern of the two east entrance towers, with the well.*

which may even have been wrought by the Stewarts themselves in support of Robert Bruce, the purpose being to deny the fortress to the advancing English. Evidence was found that the English had nevertheless occupied the slighted castle, rebuilding the east gatehouse towers in timber. It is interesting to note that earth-and-timber fortifications achieved a new currency during the Wars of Independence, as they were quick and cheap to build. There was further evidence that the site was then attacked and destroyed by the Scots in the early years of the fourteenth century; the base of the towers had been levelled, sealing the remains of burnt timbers.

Robert Stewart was crowned Robert II in 1371, and soon afterwards he ordered the

rebuilding of Dundonald in the nascent style of his day: the tower house. This was built on the site of the west towers of the thirteenth-century castle, with a barmkin enclosed to the east, creating a defensive circuit on a more modest scale. Access was now via both a gate on the north side of the tower, and by the ancient east route through the barmkin wall. The enclosed space was naturally divided by the contours into a higher outer court, entered by the east gate, and a lower inner court, which stood immediately in front of the tower. Excavations showed that the outer court contained poorly built storage and stable ranges, along with a large, rock-cut water cistern that replaced the old east well which was now outwith the enclosure.

The planning of the inner court was determined by the location of the pre-existing chapel; this was cleverly used to create a narrow entrance to the inner sanctum, which then allowed access to the tower forestair. At the same time this enabled a direct link to be formed between the tower and the chapel by means of a passage which oversailed the inner entrance.

Spynie Palace

The development of Spynie (Moray) makes an interesting comparison to that of Dundonald, as this also began as an earthwork, possibly being transformed into a stone (or partly stone) enclosure castle in the thirteenth century, and then being comprehensively rebuilt in the following two centuries.

The excavations have shown that the defended enclosure at Spynie might originally have been constructed in the late twelfth century, possibly during the revolt of the MacWilliams *c*. 1187. The site was of considerable strategic importance, being on a loch which gave direct access to the sea, 5km (3 miles) away to the north. At this time the site was probably a ringwork, comprising an earth bank which enclosed a number of timber buildings. A shallow ditch outwith the south range produced pottery of twelfth-century date.

In the early thirteenth century this became the palace of Bishop Bricius when he made the nearby church of Holy Trinity his cathedral. In 1224 the cathedral was fixed at Elgin, but Spynie remained the principal residence. This wealthy place acted as a focus for trade, and a community grew up in the shadow of the palace. In the mid-thirteenth century the earthwork castle was partly transformed with the addition of at least two stone buildings revealed by the excavations. One was located beneath the great fifteenth-century tower house, and had been a mural tower with at least one window of beautifully painted glass, produced by the same glaziers who were employed at Elgin Cathedral. Very close to this was a small, stone-built, free-standing building, which was probably a kitchen (84).

The site was then abandoned for about fifty years, before being rebuilt entirely in stone, commencing in the early decades of the fourteenth century. By now the entrance was through the ground floor of the south range, facing a northern postern or watergate entrance. The stone tower at the south-west corner was possibly replaced by a large, circular mural tower, and this may have been matched by smaller towers at each of the other three corners.

The plan was further revised during the late fifteenth and into the sixteenth century, at the instigation of Bishop David Stewart. He gave his name to the massive tower house, with accommodation on six floors, which replaced the circular corner tower. The south gate was blocked and a new gateway constructed,

84 Spynie; looking south, with the great tower house (right), and earlier kitchen (centre).

which faced east into the likely site of the burgh. By now there were ranges against all four walls, no doubt providing service, storage, bedroom and dining-space in addition to the large amount of space stacked in the tower house. The north range was rebuilt in a spectacular fashion, divided in two at ground level by a new watergate. To the west at this level were kitchens, separated by the watergate passage from storage space and the main well in the east basement. On the floor above was the banqueting hall; this was a huge space, measuring 27m (89ft) by 10m (33ft), with the dais at the east end, and a screen at the west end which hid from view the final preparation of dishes.

Edinburgh Castle

If all Scottish castles have a mythic quality which acts as a barrier to achieving a real understanding, then Edinburgh Castle is the most extreme case. Indeed until recently we have only had a limited comprehension of how this royal fortress looked in medieval times; as at Spynie, this is due to wholesale rebuilding, caused and compounded by the scouring effects of numerous sieges. The situation is much happier now following the publication of a volume in this series which fully traces the development of Edinburgh Castle. Nevertheless, the site is so vast that the recent excavations have only been able to open up some keyholes, which even in relatively large areas account for less than 1 per cent of the total enclosure.

The results of the excavation of the fourteenth-century smithy are featured here in the survey of industries (p. 76); this was located on Mills Mount, a lower, northern ward which was far enough away from the royal apartments on the citadel to be an ideal location for various noxious activities. This had formed part of the Iron Age fort, and the area had continued to be occupied and used chiefly as a midden into the eleventh century.

At this time a stone causeway was laid across what must have become a smelly quagmire. The causeway was eventually engulfed by further dumps of rubbish, and from the twelfth century onwards this area was used for ironworking.

The location of the excavations was dictated by the construction of the two ends of a vehicle tunnel; Mills Mount was at the west end, while the east end was located just to the north of the current main entrance. Not surprisingly, features related to the medieval entrance and defences were found here, including a small part of two massive infilled ditches, 15m (50ft) wide by 5m (17ft) deep. These contained pottery of the thirteenth or fourteenth century, although the ditches could well be prehistoric in origin. Even more tantalizing were clues from the area just inside the ditches, which indicated that the medieval entrance had been here, rather than on the higher level it is today. Parts of a blocked entrance were found in a wall which had originally extended much further to enclose a levelled platform in what is now Princes Street Gardens. Fragments of an inner gatehouse were found within this bastion, which was reduced in size in the early seventeenth century and adapted for artillery use.

These small excavations in outer parts of Edinburgh Castle have highlighted the great potential that exists here for future archaeological investigations which could unlock some of the mysteries concerning the medieval buildings. There is, for example, the fascinating suggestion that St Margaret's Chapel may have formed an integral element of a Norman keep, built by David I in the 1120s. One million visitors each year do, however, represent a major impediment to digging large holes in the ground!

Threave Castle

The excavations at Threave (Kirkcudbright) in the mid-1970s ushered in the new era of castle

85 Excavation of one of the lost fourteenth-century halls at Threave. The tower house is enclosed by fifteenth-century artillery defences.

investigations. These were not so much concerned with the main tower, but instead focused on the practical functioning of the castle in the context of the development of the defences.

This is a secure island site in the River Dee, and like Cruggleton and Dundonald played an important role in the defence of the western marches of the kingdom. Also like Cruggleton, this was probably a fortification of the lords of Galloway during the twelfth and thirteenth centuries, although little of the early earthwork castle was found during the excavations. In 1369 the site came into the possession of the Black Douglases, through the marvellously named Archibald the Grim, Lord of Galloway, who had the great tower house built. This contained the earl's main lodging, with a hall

in the middle, kitchens and storage below, and private chambers above. The excavations revealed, however, that the apparently solitary tower house did not stand alone, but had been fronted by two large halls, which stood 50m (165ft) to the east of the entrance to the tower. These stone halls were both at least two storeys high and were about 22m (73ft) in length, with one at right angles to the other. They were probably equipped with kitchens and service accommodation on the ground floor, and private chambers above. The southern of the two was L-shaped in plan, with an annexe which may have contained a chapel. The plan of this hall block bore a marked resemblance to that of another Douglas castle at Bothwell (Lanark) (85).

A group of workshop buildings was found to the south of the halls, and the evidence showed that the occupants were skilled in wood-turning, and in the working of iron, lead and leather. Pottery was scarce, and other

86 *Paddle and wooden bowls from the harbour at Threave.*

87 *Harbour gate-post, Threave.*

materials, especially wood, were used instead (**86**). One of the bowls was stamped with a heart, the emblem of the Douglases. The most remarkable discoveries were made in the small harbour, which survived on the west side of the tower. This had become silted, leaving the deposits in the harbour waterlogged, and so the preservation of organic material was excellent. The harbour was D-shaped in plan, and enclosed by stone walls on all but part of the landward east side, where a post-and-wattle wall was found. The narrow harbour mouth was closed with a gate, and one of the gate posts was found *in situ* (**87**). Preserved in the harbour mud were boat parts, shoes, scabbards, crossbow bolts and even a barrel full of gunstones: ammunition for early artillery. The organic content was no doubt boosted by effluent from one of the tower garderobes which was flushed into the

88 Threave; harbour during excavation.

harbour (**88**)!

The food debris indicated that a sophisticated standard of animal husbandry was practised on the nearby estates, with sheep and cattle being slaughtered at the optimum age for meat production. The diet was varied and included red deer from hunting, along with domestic fowl and geese. Curlew and gull bones were also found, as were the remains of cats and dogs including a large hunting hound, which stood taller than a modern Alsatian.

Troubled times lay ahead for this great aristocratic family, presaged by the construction *c.* 1450 of a great artillery wall and ditch, which necessitated the destruction of the two residential halls. The family retreated behind these walls, but the quarrel with James II led to the murder in 1452 of the eighth earl, by the king's own hand. Threave was besieged and fell due to treachery, not force, in 1455, leading to the destruction of the Black Douglas family.

Smailholm

Smailholm Tower (Roxburgh) is at the opposite end of the scale to Threave, and yet the same archaeological strategy has been applied here to good effect (**89**). The castle was built in the fifteenth century by the Pringles, who were lesser lairds with sizeable border estates. They served as 'Rangers', helping to administer part of the royal forest of Ettrick. The craggy castle site was the 'mains' or home farm of this branch of the Pringles. A survey of the surrounding area revealed three groups of farm buildings, and the remains of a stable block located just outside the main entrance through the west barmkin wall of the castle. A millpond was recorded a short distance to the east of the tower.

The excavations revealed that the otherwise cramped accommodation provided by the

105

89 *Smailholm: reconstruction of the fifteenth-century tower house and barmkin.*

tower house had always been augmented by a second residential unit, built of stone, adjoining the north-west corner of the tower. This comprised a single-storey hall with a central fireplace and a separate chamber. Facing this across a stone-slabbed courtyard was another range, which was a kitchen with a brewhouse or bakehouse. All the walls were clay-bonded, and the roofs were of turf or thatch, unlike the tower which was roofed in stone. There was probably no kitchen in the tower, and so family meals may have been prepared in the tower-hall fireplace.

Eyemouth Fort

The middle years of the sixteenth century were a time of great political and military upheavals, with the English once again trying to gain control over Scotland, to thus destroy the alliance between the Scots and the French which posed the threat of invasion by way of England's 'back door'. After twenty years of peace the intense military activity of the 1540s brought about the introduction of radical new artillery fortifications, which utilized Italianate designs. High stone towers were no longer an

adequate defence against, or platform for, the improved guns. So a whole new foreign vocabulary of fortifications was learnt, based upon the principle of creating sharply angled gun batteries out of earth with timber-and-stone facings. These ramparts could absorb incoming fire while presenting a low profile to the enemy gunners.

Such a fort was built by the English in 1547 on a coastal promontory at Eyemouth (Berwickshire) (**90**). This formed part of the strategy of Protector Somerset to create a secure buffer zone in southern Scotland, defended by a series of great artillery forts. The main frontal element of the fort was a massive earthen rampart, with a ditch and counterscarp bank, which cut off the promontory. Projecting out to the front of the rampart was an angle-pointed bastion, known as the 'King's Work', a sort of diamond-shaped bulwark. The entrance was to the south of this.

The excavations revealed that the 4m (13ft) high rampart was constructed of earth with a stepped profile reinforced with turf, and finished with a smooth profile of clay. The bastion was further protected with a masonry cladding. A pattern of nails on the top of the rampart showed where a prefabricated light superstructure of timber stood; this was essential for providing protection for the gunners due to the low height and gentle gradients of the fortifications. The ramparts were hollow in places to accommodate lower gun positions, known as casemates, which provided lethal flanking fire along the face of the bastion. These casemates created a dangerous weakness, however, because an attack might cause the rampart above to collapse. A contemporary plan of the site indicated to the excavators where some of the main buildings might be found on the enclosed promontory. One of these was the English captains' lodging, which was found to be 9m (30ft) long, with steps down at the entrance, and with a large fireplace and plastered walls inside. Although clearly built to last, the fort was abandoned and partially demolished in 1550.

The site was refortified in 1557 by the French, under orders from Mary of Guise, Queen Dowager and widow of James V. The excavations showed that the French further extended the frontal defences by building a great rampart and ditch with a pair of end bastions in front of the English rampart. The King's Work was repaired and the stone cladding replaced, creating a platform for guns which fired over the new front rampart. After only two years the English negotiated the removal of the French, stipulating that the fort had to be levelled. This was done, although substantial earthworks can still be seen today.

For all their sophistication, the basic military need behind the construction of these forts – to create effective defences quickly and cheaply – was not new. This was the same driving force behind the Edwardian timber peles built during the Wars of Independence, and the earthwork castles of the century and a half before then. Of more significance was the fact that these Italianate forts were not to be the homes of nobles, but rather military bases for the first recognizably professional armies. Moreover, the advances in the technology of artillery helped bring about the decline of the castle in favour of country residences with greater emphasis on comfort.

90 *Reconstruction of the English fort at Eyemouth.*

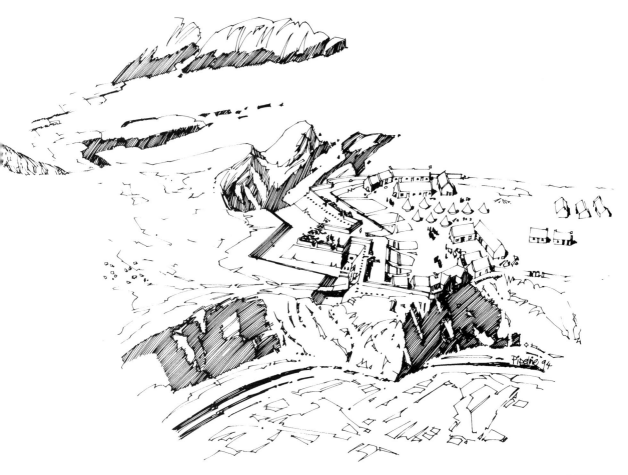

CHAPTER EIGHT

Rural settlement

The invisible centuries in the Scottish countryside

The archaeology of the medieval farming communities is one of the greatest mysteries of our past; we understand very little of life in the countryside, and yet even by the sixteenth century this was where 90 per cent of the population lived and toiled. Agriculture and settlement were ubiquitous, and yet no typical medieval farm has ever been excavated, either in the Highlands or in the Lowlands. The rural landscapes of today effectively mask the medieval farms, fields and mills, chiefly because of the agricultural 'improving' movement of the eighteenth and nineteenth centuries. The grassy foundations of deserted sites can be found on the upland margins, but dating these sites on form alone is impossible.

The evidence is there but is hidden, and consequently much has to be made of the data retrieved from the burghs concerning the products of the countryside (p. 66). This has to be coupled with insights gained from the excavation of the few sites which have attracted the attention of archaeologists, firstly because they are visible, and secondly because they possess some qualities of 'specialness'. We are fortunate, however, in having some very good general data produced by field survey. The overall lack of excavated evidence inevitably means that this chapter must include more general comments derived from

the work of historians and geographers.

The settlements

Dispersed farming settlements, known as 'fermtouns', existed throughout most of southern, central and eastern Scotland. These were home for four to eight families of tenants, jointly contributing draught oxen or horses to a shared team. A fermtoun was enclosed and consisted of a number of farmhouses usually of 'longhouse' type, that is, divided into two or three rooms with animals kept in one end during the winter. An especially long building might have contained a threshing barn, with large opposed entrances so as to create a through-draught to carry off the chaff. In addition there would be barns, byres, stores, yards and pens, along with smaller cottages for labourers. Settlements were scattered, and villages did not exist as we know them today (91).

Lowland fermtouns were surrounded by the constantly cultivated infield strip fields, with some hay meadows nearby. In turn these core fields were enclosed by a 'head dyke', a stony bank beyond which was the occasionally cultivated outfield and areas of rough grazing. The situation was different in the Highlands, as explored in the survey of north-east Perthshire published by the RCAHMS, where fermtouns in the glens were found to be sited on a linear head dyke, which ran along a break in the

91 *Wardhouse, Aberdeenshire; sinuous rig fields radiating out from the fermtoun, with prehistoric clearance cairns and roundhouses beyond.*

slope at the margin between the infield and the rough hill grazing. At the Spittal of Glenshee (Perthshire) complete pre-improvement landscapes have been discovered, with the head dyke running along the 370m (1220ft) contour (**colour plate 14**). The deserted fermtouns on both sides of the valley were probably seventeenth or eighteenth century in date, but these farmers had utilized house platforms, rigs and cultivation terraces originally created in the medieval period. The same survey also identified a new type of early medieval small farm known as 'Pitcarmick-type' after the place they were first found, based on a single longhouse with rounded corners and bowed sides. These houses have a separate distribution away from the glen-side

fermtouns, but close to the prehistoric hut-circle groups. Excavations in 1994 indicated a medieval date for one site, and it is possible that these are the 'missing link' between the Iron Age farms and the later fermtouns.

Fields

Old rig-and-furrow fields can be found in many parts of Scotland, either surviving above ground in upland areas, or else as crop marks where they have long been ploughed flat. Each rig was an individual strip field, which the plough-team of horses and/or oxen could plough in a day. Rigs often have a sinuous, reversed S shape created by the repeated action of the heavy mould-board plough. This may have been introduced along with other agricultural innovations by the new monastic landlords in the twelfth century. The strip fields were arranged in contiguous blocks, with each rig being an average width of 4.5m

92 *Medieval farmer's toolkit.*

the 'lazy-bed', which were isolated blocks of short rigs created with a spade; these are found in upland areas. The spade was an essential part of the limited toolkit of the medieval farmer, along with the hoe, sickle and scythe. The spade was usually made of wood with an attached iron blade (**92**).

Environment and society

By the twelfth century, man had already been clearing woodland and creating fields for thousands of years, and yet significant areas of woodland remained, and much of the lower-lying land was too boggy to be farmed, hence the need to farm at heights no longer considered feasible today. This situation can be further explained when set in the context of the contemporary climatic and environmental conditions. Times were good between 1000 and 1200 thanks to a warmer climate, which allowed higher cultivation heights and the northerly growing of wheat. During this time Kelso Abbey had a grange (monastic farm) at 300m (1000ft), with 1400 sheep, 16 shepherds' cottages and 100ha (250 acres) of tillage. This phase of warm climate and good harvests spanned the period of the creation of great feudal estates and monastic sheep farms, and it is not surprising that this led to a rise in population, with more farming settlements being established and more woodland being cleared.

Things changed for the worse after *c.* 1300 when the climate deteriorated for almost five centuries, to create the era known as the Mini Ice Age. This time of cold winters and bad summers, strong winds and heavy rains, resulted in frequent episodes of crop failure and famine. Coastal sand-blow disasters destroyed whole settlements, as recorded at Forvie (Moray) in October 1413, when the sand advanced 250m (830ft). During the fourteenth century this must have seemed a very sudden change compared to the times of recent memory, and of course the effect on the

(15ft). Experiments have shown that ridged fields can be easily created by ploughing over a period of just a few years. Rigs were needed in areas of heavy rainfall with poor-quality, badly drained soils, as the ridging process created a greater depth of soil, combined with better drainage downslope along the furrow.

But these were not the only field systems; ridging would have been unnecessary in the well-drained parts of the Lowlands prior to the climatic deterioration of the late thirteenth century. Investigations in the gravel areas of Fife and Angus have discovered large, flat, open fields, enclosed by widely spaced, parallel boundary ditches, sealed beneath later medieval rig systems. Another type of field is population was made even worse by the decades of sporadic war with England, coupled with the first outbreaks of plague.

Plague probably killed one in three of the population, being proportionately worse in the south of Scotland compared to the colder north, where the fleas and rats found it harder to thrive. Fewer people inevitably meant that rents were lowered while labour costs rose, with less land being ploughed by a peasantry comprised of many more free husbandmen than existed before.

Economy and food

The countryside was where the wealth of the nation was created, the principal raw materials being sheep and cattle. At the height of the export trade, in the fourteenth century, the clip of about two million sheep along with the hides of some 50,000 cattle were shipped each year through the burgh ports. These beasts, however, were not what sustained the farmers and their families; they existed chiefly on the products of cereal production, that is, oatmeal and ale, along with dairy products, meat, fish and kail. There is good evidence to suggest that the milk came from sheep and goats, as seen in the bone assemblage from the excavations of the coastal settlement and manorial castle at Rattray (Moray). Here, cattle were the main meat-producing species, being slaughtered at the optimum age for producing meat and good leather hides. By contrast the sheep were quite old, being kept for their annual crop of wool and their milk. It is likely that younger sheep, missing from the bone assemblage, were exported by boat to the meat market in Aberdeen. The pigs kept at Rattray were eaten young, when most succulent, rather than when they reached optimum weight. The coastal location meant that the inhabitants could also exploit the marine environment for food, as represented by the bones of seals as well as a considerable amount of fish. Whale, porpoise and dolphin

were also eaten, probably as a result of chance strandings.

The majority of rural settlements, including Rattray, relied on a mixed economy of pastoral and arable farming. Oats and bere (a kind of barley) were the basic crops, along with some bread-wheat and rye. Corn-drying kilns have been found, very similar to those excavated in Perth (p. 74), and these would have been a common feature of the fermtouns, their function being to prepare corn for milling, or storage as seed corn, or else as part of the malting process. Domestic hand-querns have also been found, although bulk processing was done at the lord's mill. Mills were small and powered by water turning either a vertical or horizontal wheel. Again relying on the evidence from the burghs, cash crops such as flax and hemp were also important. Cash crops and surpluses, grown during the times of peace and better weather, meant that some large sections of the peasantry could be well-off, which goes against a widely held belief that life for the country folk was universally grim. Another fallacy is that of the mass autumn slaughter, now dispelled by the ages of animals found in the burghs. Stock were overwintered, being fed on hay, straw from threshing, kail stalks and leaf fodder, while being sheltered in byres and longhouses.

Specialist non-agricultural communities also existed, a good example being the fishing settlement at Eyemouth (Berwickshire). Excavations in the rivermouth area discovered the midden, which was a mixture of domestic and fish-processing waste, the contents of which helped to reconstruct the economy of the settlement from the twelfth to the fifteenth century. Fish was the main element of the diet, with the surplus being sold on. Many species were represented especially cod, ling, haddock (which were caught in the winter and spring) and herring (caught in the summer and autumn). Some deposits contained just the heads and upper vertebrae of cod and ling, representing waste from the preparation of

93 Rattray; thirteenth/fourteenth-century industrial zone looking north. The potting tenement with kilns divided by the central line of the stream from the smithy.

carcasses for salting. The resulting dried cod was popular in the burghs and monasteries. Herring were simply gutted before being smoked, or salted and then packed in barrels. Barrels of fish appear in the documentary record as an important export. The investigation showed that the fisherfolk were keeping some sheep for wool, and some mature cattle for traction and dairying, but the most important activity was fishing.

Industry

All the crafts and industries found in the burghs originated in the countryside, and these continued to be an important part of the rural economy, some on a domestic scale and others on a commercial scale. All raw materials were of course rural products, pre-eminent among which was iron. Iron ore was obtained as 'bog ore' from peated-up lochs, and smelted close to where it was found. The ore was smelted on the lochside, and when

one bog was exhausted they would simply move on to the next and build a new furnace. These smelters produced raw iron, known as 'blooms'. This was a seasonal activity probably done in the summer by smiths and farmers, when the bogs were comparatively dry. Large-scale production is best known from Rannoch Moor in highland Perthshire, but other sites are also known, for example in Lanarkshire, where smelting was done for domestic consumption rather than as a fully commercial industry.

All rural populations needed access to a blacksmith who could manufacture and repair farming implements. A smithy was found at Rattray, alongside a pottery, within a central industrial zone midway between the castle and the church. The smithy was divided from the pottery by a stream which provided the water for both industries. The furnace was not discovered, but a timber-framed workshop was found, which measured 5m (17ft) by 12m (40ft). Most of the debris was from the refining of blooms and the manufacture and repair of tools and other objects. The furnace was fuelled with coal which was shipped to the settlement from central Scotland, probably via Aberdeen (**93**).

112

This industrial zone at Rattray was busiest in the thirteenth and fourteenth centuries. Like the smithy next door, the pottery consisted of an enclosed property with timber buildings and open yards. The excavations revealed all the essential features of a potting tenement: access to clay and water on site, kilns, clay storage and preparation facilities, and a workshop/store. A number of small kilns were replaced by a single larger one in the fourteenth century. This was oval in plan, with a chamber which was *c*. 2m (6ft) long. The base was recessed into the ground and was revetted with rough stonework; it had twin opposed flues so it could be stoked with peat fuel from either side. The full load was estimated to be about sixty wheel-thrown pots of different sizes. Once stacked, the pots were covered with a layer of peats or turfs, which was in turn sealed under a layer of clay, leaving some vent-holes. The products were also found, having been used in the castle and settlement; these were mainly jugs, jars and bowls with splashes of green glaze. It seems likely that production was small scale and aimed chiefly at this community, with potting therefore being a seasonal activity and the kiln fired only a few times a year.

Kilns located closer to large centres of population in eastern Scotland were producing pottery on a much larger scale, although very few production sites have been found. A group of kilns was being used by potters in the thirteenth and fourteenth centuries at Colstoun near Haddington. Large quantities of jugs and globular cooking pots were manufactured here and traded throughout the region.

Forests and deer parks

Hunting was the foremost recreation of the king and the nobility. Numerous hunting reserves were created in this heavily forested land by David I and his successors, being held directly by the crown or else by barons and churchmen. These areas were meant to be kept free of settlement and agriculture, and yet some were encroached on during and after the thirteenth century as pressure on land increased. Consequently during the fourteenth century smaller deer parks were created, a good example being Buzzart Dykes (Perthshire) sited on the fringe of the royal forest of Clunie. An area of 86ha (212 acres) was enclosed with a bank and internal ditch, so designed as to allow deer in but not to let them escape (**colour plate 15**). Hunting reserves were controlled by forest officers, and their homes and the lordly hunting-lodges may be identified in or around the forests.

The right to cut timber was jealously guarded by the crown and lords; we have seen in the evidence from the excavations in Perth that timber for building was being obtained from the immediate hinterland in an opportunistic, unmanaged fashion (p. 69). On the other hand there is documentary evidence for the sustainable management of woodland by the proprietors, with practices such as coppicing and regeneration being employed. Nevertheless, there were serious timber shortages from the fifteenth century on, with large quantities being imported from the Baltic.

Granges – the monks' breadbasket

The wave of piety which swept Europe in the twelfth century washed up a large number of new monastic foundations on Scottish shores, all of which needed substantial, ongoing economic support to survive. Large parts of royal estates were transferred into monastic ownership, and these provided food and rents. They also developed their own farms which were known as 'granges'; this is a common place-name in the vicinity of monasteries, showing where these medieval farms existed. The Cistercians were more extreme than others, in that to achieve seclusion and self-sufficiency they aimed to have large, consolidated properties, farmed directly by their lay brothers and labourers. This sometimes meant the removal of existing fermtouns and their inhabitants. This would have happened on the estates of the Cistercians of Coupar Angus (Perthshire), who were responsible for the first major land-reclamation projects, when they drained much of the Carse of Gowrie between 1170 and 1230 to create a large expanse of open fields. The site of Coupar Grange has been identified as a crop mark of a substantial rectilinear ditched enclosure containing a number of large, rectangular timber buildings. It is known that such a complex would have: a chapel, main barn, stables, seed house, kitchen, brewhouse, bakehouse, mill, dovecot and fish-ponds (94).

The drastic changes of the fourteenth century made it difficult for the abbeys to maintain their estates in the same way, and

94 *Crop marks of timber buildings at Coupar Grange.*

increasingly grange lands were leased to secular tenants.

Springwood Park

This farming settlement was located in rich arable land *c.* 1km (1200yds) to the south of the medieval burgh and royal castle of Roxburgh, on the estate of the Maxwell lords close to Kelso Abbey. Excavations revealed a group of terraced farm cottages laid out along a road, which had formed part of a larger settlement, near to the site of a bridge over the River Teviot. A complex sequence of building was revealed, dated from the twelfth to fourteenth centuries by a rich assemblage of coins and pottery.

Three phases of timber cottages were found facing on to the road, culminating in the mid-thirteenth century with the construction of a conjoined terrace of three houses, each approximately 4m (13ft) wide by 10m (33ft) long. These were cruck-roofed houses, with heather-thatched roofs and cobbled floors with stone-lined drains. Structural ironwork was found which had come from framed door-ways. The earlier simple cottages had been replaced by longhouses, each with a byre at the down-slope end, allowing effluent to drain away (**95**). The farmers were growing oats, barley, wheat and rye, as well as keeping cattle and some sheep. The discovery of horseshoes and harness fittings showed that they owned horses. This rich agricultural economy was augmented by other activities including domestic cloth production, as represented by the discovery of a heckle, spindle whorls and loom weights; and cheesemaking, represented by a pot base which had been transformed into a strainer.

The suggestion that these folk were tenants is upheld by the fact that their very regular buildings were rearranged on two separate occasions, indicating central planning at the behest of a superior. This was a rural settlement much in the shadow of the nearby royal, burghal and monastic centres of

95 Reconstruction of thirteenth-century longhouses at Springwood Park.

consumption. Most of the rural settlements in the eastern heartland were similarly close to such centres. These rich markets encouraged the farmers to create a surplus, payment for which was represented by the silver coins and other artefacts found at Springwood.

Rattray – a rural burgh

The farmers at Rattray flourished between the thirteenth and fifteenth centuries under the shadow of the manorial castle (p. 93) at the east end of the settlement. The church was located 550m (600yds) west of the castle, and the settlement grew up between the two, reminiscent of an urban plan. Indeed, in the thirteenth century Rattray was legally defined as a burgh of barony, and therefore a town; yet the excavations showed that the small population were dependent on agriculture and fishing, making this a rural settlement (**96**).

Timber houses were laid out on either side of a single road, in an apparently urban manner, each house within its own rectangular plot of land and each separated by boundary ditches. Central to the settlement were the two largest properties which contained the smithy and the pottery (p. 113). A handful of other buildings were also excavated: those built in the thirteenth century were of timber-and-turf construction, whereas those built in the following century had thick clay walls with clay-bonded stone gable ends. Could this heavier construction reflect the colder times of the fourteenth century? On the landward side the settlement was enclosed by arable and common lands. Part of the rig-and-furrow was detected, and excavation here revealed that the light sandy soil had been manured with the rubbish from the settlement. A salt-marsh divided the properties from the lochside to the north, and in the summer this would have been used as grazing land.

Other specialist crafts were represented in the finds from the excavations, including woodworkers' and masons' tools. The discovery of the seal matrix of William the Cooper showed that a barrelmaker was also employed here in the fourteenth century. The economic base was weak, however, and evidence was found of rapid decline after the manor was abandoned in the fifteenth century.

Finlaggan – a western capital

Finlaggan (Argyll) has long been identified as the capital of the MacDonald Lords of the Isles, but it is only the excavations in the 1990s which are providing the first real understanding of medieval life in and around the Western Isles. The Norse and Gaels created a distinctive culture which persisted and was far removed from that of the south and east; it is not surprising that this was to lead to conflict.

Finlaggan is located in a freshwater loch in the middle of Islay. It was close to some of the best farmland in the west, with materials such as timber and lead ore. The site had an administrative and religious importance stretching back to prehistoric and early Christian times, so the inherent power of the site itself was no doubt embedded in the minds of many generations. The loch provided an ideal natural defence protecting the two islands – Eilean Mor (the Great Island) (**colour plate 16**) and Eilean na Comhairle (the Council Island). The main period of importance was during the fourteenth and fifteenth centuries, but the excavations have shown that there were earlier phases of defences on the Council Island including a thirteenth-century stone castle. The castle was probably destroyed during the Wars of Independence, but the fortunes of the MacDonalds recovered soon after, having supported the Bruce cause. Before the excavations began the only standing structure on the site was the chapel.

96 *Rattray; reconstruction of the motte, church and settlement in the thirteenth century* (after J. Dunbar).

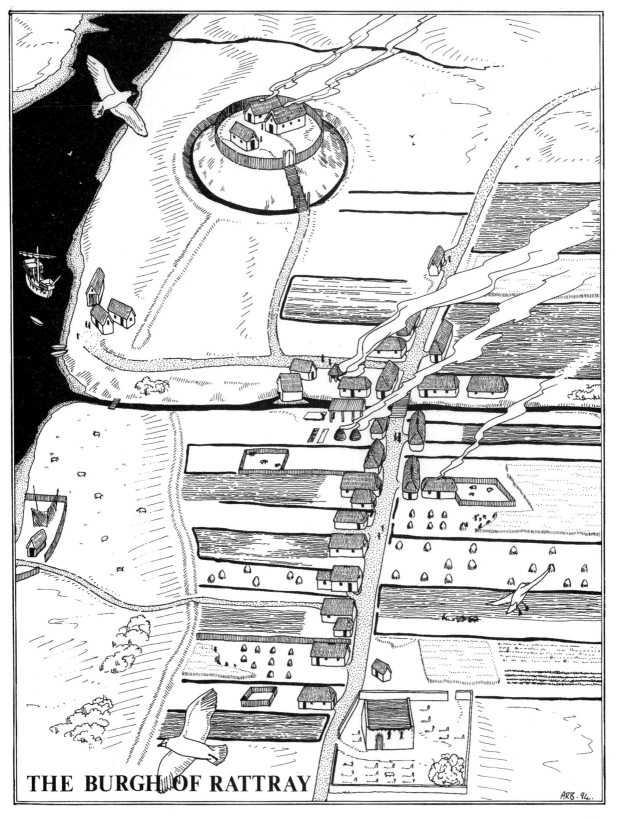

THE BURGH OF RATTRAY

97 *Discovery of the cross-head, Finlaggan.*

The island could be approached by a causeway, or by boat, both giving access to the north side. The east part of the island was enclosed by a turf-and-stone bank which was faced with stone and revetted with timber. This may have served a dual purpose not only as a defensive barrier, but also acting as a stock enclosure. Having been admitted through an entrance in the bank the visitor then walked along cobbled roads, past a long line of buildings which faced gable-on to the road. At the east end of the main group of these was the chapel. Excavations around this revealed the rectangular stone base for a cross, and the excavators were amazed to discover the carved stone head of the cross nearby, dating from *c.* 1400 (**97, 98**).

Various house types were found, but most were of cruck construction, and measured an average of 6m (20ft) by 12m (40ft), with timber, turf or clay superstructures and thatched roofs. There were clear signs of Norse ancestry in the house designs, especially in those which had stone sub-basements, sprung wooden floors and timber super-structures. The road led past these to the Great Hall which was almost 20m (66ft) in length, with an impressive open roof, supported on stone corbels carved in the form of human heads. Kitchens next to the Great Hall produced evidence of catering on a grand scale. Access from here to the Council Island was by another causeway; the excavations have shown that this island is artificial, being formed from the debris of successive phases of building, spanning more than one thousand years. The final phases consisted of three buildings, the largest of which was probably the actual chamber where the Council of the Isles met. The other two buildings have been identified as the hall and kitchen of the MacDonald lords. The artefacts revealed that specialist craftsmen and metalworkers were employed here. Harp-pins, used to keep the strings tight, along with the evidence for food preparation, all help conjure up an image of great feasts, which would have taken place the few times a year when the Council met. This was a place of ceremony, justice and govern-ment, functions which were interlinked with the consumption and redistribution of food and other commodities. Some of the roadside

98 *Cross-head (one-eighth scale) from Finlaggan.*

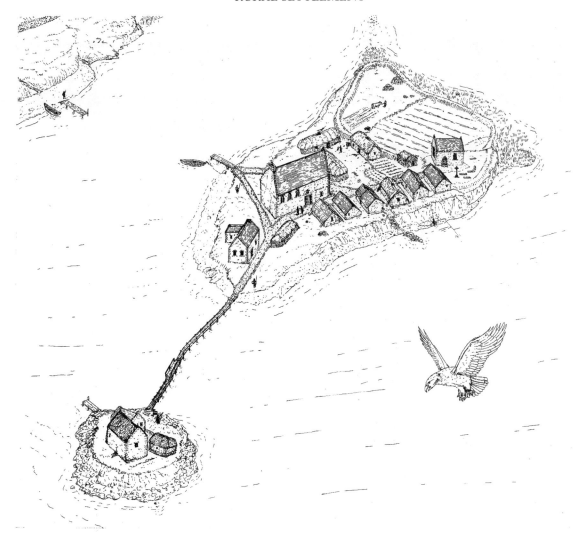

99 *Finlaggan; reconstruction of the site in the fifteenth century.*

houses would therefore have been stores and guest-houses (**99**).

The MacDonalds were powerful lords who posed a threat to the Stewart dynasty, a situation which was resolved in 1493 by the crushing of the family along with the forfeiture of their lands. The excavations have shown that all the main buildings were destroyed at this time, and the site put over to low-status agricultural use, finally drawing a veil over what had been one of the most important ritual and ceremonial centres in the west.

Kebister – a teind barn on Shetland

Teind (tithe) barns were a common feature of the medieval landscape, and this is the only one which has been excavated. Its function and ownership would certainly have remained anonymous but for the fortunate discovery of the armorial stone which was found where it had fallen from above the door. The stone is identified with Henry Phankouth who was Archdeacon of Shetland from 1501 until 1529; this was an influential office in the diocese of Orkney. His position entitled him to teinds (income from churches) and rents from numerous properties, which were paid in butter, oil and cloth. These would have been

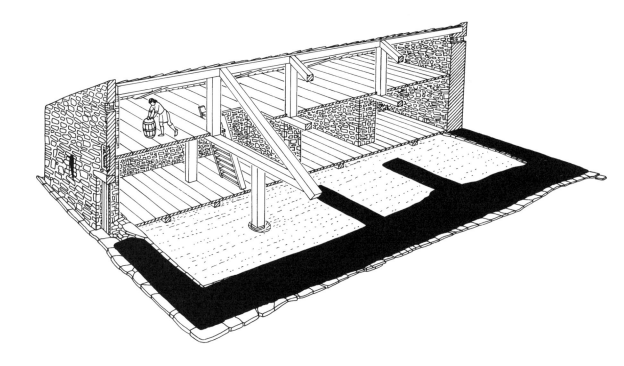

100 *Reconstruction of the Kebister teind barn, Shetland.*

stored in this two-storey, stone-built barn, before being sold on for cash.

The excavations revealed the base of a 17m (57ft) long barn, with access through a single entrance in the west gable (**100**). It had a sprung timber floor at ground level and was roofed with stone slabs. The armorial stone was of such high-quality carving that it must have been done by masons working on the cathedral at Kirkwall. It occupied a prominent position above the door; the ostentatious heraldry was no doubt intended to help discourage unlawful entry.

Afterword: a future for the medieval past

Much has been learnt, and it is exciting to consider that even more time capsules of medieval life await discovery. Very few discoveries are made by chance, and most come about as a result of careful stewardship of the historic environment. We can all help to ensure that potentially important sites, and the irreplaceable data and artefacts they contain, are saved by contacting local authority archaeologists or Historic Scotland when any

101 *Rescue archaeology in Perth: the pleasures of winter digging.*

site is threatened by damage or erosion.

Great strides forward have been made in understanding the archaeology of some of the larger burghs, but as we have seen, these were home to less than 10 per cent of the population. To fully understand the development of medieval life and culture we must look to the land. I have been able to say little about the west, the north and the islands, as so few excavations have taken place there. Integrated rural studies are required, a number of which should be spread around the various regions. These studies should combine environmental, historical and place-name approaches with archaeological field survey and excavation. The techniques of medieval farming could be better understood if put to the test in experimental farms, as has been successfully achieved in Scandinavia.

Environmental archaeology has made an enormous contribution to our comprehension of life, allowing past environments, diet and economy to be reconstructed in great detail. This is markedly the case in Perth, where conditions are favourable for the preservation of much organic material. Even more can be learnt from the excavation of such sites in Perth and elsewhere, and these should be targeted whenever they become available during the course of redevelopment. Large-scale rebuilding within historic burghs may have ceased, however, increasing the value of the hard-won data already recovered from hurried rescue excavations of the 1970s and 1980s, often done perforce during the winter months (**101**).

The healthy state of the archaeological study of this period is reflected in the handful of carefully tailored research projects underway (mid-1990s) at Whithorn, Finlaggan, Pitcarmick and on the Isle of May. In each case the results are informing us not only about the specific sites, but more importantly helping create a much clearer picture of the lives of all sections of medieval society.

There can be no doubt that medieval life was hard and for most was (mercifully) short. But by the same token I have been keen to dispel the myth that this was a time of unmitigated misery – we only have to look at the evidence from Perth in the twelfth century to see that life could be good. Generally, this was a period of growth: growth of population, growth of settlements and growth of an assured national identity, as expressed clearly to us even today through the buildings that survive. And this took place against a background of intermittent warfare, pestilence and famine, with a climate that was even worse than it is today!

Sites and museums to visit

Each year there are a small number of medieval excavations taking place in Scotland that can be visited. It is not possible to visit all excavations, as some are conducted at speed on building sites during the early stages of redevelopment. Information on current projects can be obtained from:

Historic Scotland
Longmore House
Salisbury Place
Edinburgh EH9 1SH

and

Council for Scottish Archaeology
c/o National Museums of Scotland
Queen Street
Edinburgh EH2 1JD

A number of museums house displays of excavated material from medieval excavations. Some of the most important artefacts are cur-rently being prepared for exhibition in the new Museum of Scotland, Chamber Street, Edinburgh, to be opened in 1998. This will include material from the excavations at the burgh of Berwick-upon-Tweed, the castles of Threave and Bothwell; the abbeys of Jedburgh and Kelso; the pottery kilns at Colstoun; and the Isle of Finlaggan.

Other important displays can be seen at the Hunterian and Kelvingrove Museums, Glasgow. Individual towns have municipal museums which feature displays of locally excavated material, including: Perth, Dum-fries, St Andrews, Huntly House (Edinburgh), Tankerness House (Orkney) and the Abbot House in Dunfermline.

Some of the sites featured in the book are in the care of Historic Scotland and have site museums, some of the most important of which are at Melrose, Arbroath and Jedburgh abbeys, and at St Andrews Cathedral. There are also site museums at Tantallon Castle and Dirleton Castle, both in East Lothian.

Further reading

Aberdeen Art Gallery and Museums *A Tale of Two Burghs*, Aberdeen, 1987.

Barrow, Geoffrey *Kingship and Unity: Scotland 1000–1306*, London, 1981.

Cruden, Stewart *The Scottish Castle*, 3rd edn, Edinburgh, 1981.

Cruden, Stewart *Scottish Medieval Churches*, Edinburgh, 1986.

Ewan, Elizabeth *Townlife in Fourteenth Century Scotland*, Edinburgh, 1990.

Fawcett, Richard *Scottish Medieval Churches*, Edinburgh, 1985.

Fawcett, Richard *Scottish Abbeys and Priories*, London, 1994.

Grant, Alexander *Independence and Nationhood: Scotland 1306–1469*, London, 1984.

Higham, Robert and Barker, Philip *Timber Castles*, London, 1992.

Holdsworth, Philip (ed.) *Excavations in the Medieval Burgh of Perth 1979–1981*, Edinburgh, 1987.

Lynch, Michael, Spearman, Michael and Stell, Geoffrey (eds) *The Scottish Medieval Town*, Edinburgh, 1988.

Ritchie, Anna *Viking Scotland*, London, 1993.

Royal Commission on the Ancient and Historical Monuments of Scotland *North-East Perth: an archaeological landscape*, Edinburgh, 1990.

Royal Commission on the Ancient and Historical Monuments of Scotland *South-East Perth: an archaeological landscape*, Edinburgh, 1994.

Stones, Judith (ed.) *Three Scottish Carmelite Friaries*, Edinburgh, 1989.

Tabraham, Chris *Scottish Castles and Fortifications*, Edinburgh, 1986.

Glossary

arcade wall Low wall supporting an interrupted line of pillars.

ashlar Tightly jointed, dressed building stone with even faces and square edges.

barmkin Walled, domestic enclosure attached to a tower-house castle.

bellcote Timber framework to mount a bell on a church roof.

bulwark Geometric-shaped bastion for mounting artillery.

buttress Vertical stone structure projecting from a wall to reinforce it, or to resist the thrust of an arch, roof or vault.

byre Animal stall or shelter.

chamfer The angled face of a lower wall foundation or moulding.

chantry chapel Privately endowed side-chapel or altar within a church, where a priest would say Masses for the soul of the deceased who made the endowment.

chapter house A grand room, close to the church, where the brethren of a monastery met daily to discuss the business of the house.

claustral Monastic buildings grouped around an open space (see **garth**), with the church forming one side of the square.

curtain-wall The main enclosing stone wall of a castle.

ecofact Organic material which informs environmental interpretation, often recovered from soil samples once excavation is complete.

effigy Sculpted representation of the deceased lying above their tomb.

finial Decorative feature on top of a roof gable.

fulling A finishing process to cleanse and thicken cloth, involving beating and steeping.

garderobe Latrine, often in a monastery or castle, usually equipped with a chute in the thickness of a stone wall.

garth Open space in the middle of a monastery cloister.

geophysical survey Process of locating buried archaeological features such as walls and ditches, by remote sensing.

kames Lead strips which held together small pieces of coloured window-glass.

lade A man-made water channel, often for a mill.

midden A domestic rubbish-heap.

minster An important early church, with an attached group of clergy.

moated site A low, square platform enclosed by a ditch and bank, forming an earth-and-timber castle or manor house.

motte An earth-and-timber castle based on a conical, flat-topped mound.

oratory Small, early medieval chapel, of earth, turf, timber, or stone.

pend A covered access between or under buildings.

presbytery The area at the east end of the church around the high altar.

reredorter A monastic toilet block, usually with direct access from the monks' dormitory.

revetment A structural reinforcement in timber or stone of a water channel or rampart.

rig A plot of land, or a strip field.

ringwork Oval or circular earthwork castle, chiefly comprising a large bank and ditch.

Romanesque Norman-influenced architectural style of the twelfth century, characterized by round-headed arches and chevron (inverted V) decoration.

shingle Wooden roof-tile.

teind The tenth-part of annual income or produce given as an offering to a parish church or monastery.

tracery Decorative stonework within a window, framing panels of plain or coloured glass.

undercroft Vaulted cellar or ground floor of a stone building.

Index

(Numbers in **bold** indicate illustrations)